MW00563438

Genesis
Series
1894

Genesis Series

1894

These Lessons were published in the Inter-Ocean Newspaper in Chicago, Illinois during the eighteen nineties.

By

Emma Curtis Hopkins

President of the Emma Curtis Hopkins Theological Seminary in Chicago, Illinois

WISEWOMAN PRESS

Genesis Series 1894

By Emma Curtis Hopkins

© WiseWoman Press 2012

Managing Editor: Michael Terranova

ISBN: 978-0945385-43-1

WiseWoman Press

Vancouver, WA 98665

www.wisewomanpress.com

www.emmacurtishopkins.com

CONTENTS

Editors Note

This is one of the few works of Emma Curtis Hopkins that doesn't follow the progression of her standard twelve lessons. These lessons were extracted from Bible Interpretation Series Eleven and Series Twelve. Each Series of Bible Interpretations represents three months of Sunday School lessons. Each lesson interprets a different Bible passage for the week, and a review of the quarter. These lessons were published weekly in the Inter-Ocean Newspaper in Chicago, Illinois in 1894.

All of Emma's other works follow the standard pattern; that of Twelve Powers, Statements, Stones, Gates, Disciples and others Twelves.

Charles Fillmore of Unity School of Christianity was ordained by The Hopkins Institute and used her teaching to create his teaching of the Twelve Powers.

Foreword

By Rev. Natalie R. Jean

I have read many teachings by Emma Curtis Hopkins, but the teachings that touch the very essence of my soul are her Bible Interpretations. There are many books written on the teachings of the Bible, but none can touch the surface of the true messages more than these Bible interpretations. With each word you can feel and see how Spirit spoke through Emma. The mystical interpretations take you on a wonderful journey to Self Realization.

Each passage opens your consciousness to a new awareness of the realities of life. The illusions of life seem to disappear through each interpretation. Emma teaches that we are the key that unlocks the doorway to the light that shines within. She incorporates ideals of other religions into her teachings, in order to understand the commonalities, so that there is a complete understanding of our Oneness. Emma opens our eyes and mind to a better today and exciting future.

Emma Curtis Hopkins, one of the Founders of New Thought teaches us to love ourselves, to speak our Truth, and to focus on our Good. My life has moved in wonderful directions because of her teachings. I know the only thing that can move me in this world is God. May these interpretations guide you to a similar path and may you truly remember that "There Is Good For You and You Ought to Have It."

Introduction

Emma Curtis Hopkins was born in 1849 in Killingly, Connecticut. She passed on April 8, 1925. Mrs. Hopkins had a marvelous education and could read many of the worlds classical texts in their original language. During her extensive studies she was always able to discover the Universal Truths in each of the world's sacred traditions. She quotes from many of these teachings in her writings. As she was a very private person, we know little about her personal life. What we do know has been gleaned from other people or from the archived writings we have been able to discover.

Emma Curtis Hopkins was one of the greatest influences on the New Thought movement in the United States. She taught over 50,000 people the Universal Truth of knowing "God is All there is." She taught many of founders of early New Thought, and in turn these individuals expanded the influence of her teachings. All of her writings encourage the student to enter into a personal relationship with God. She presses us to deny anything except the Truth of this spiritual Presence in every area of our lives. This is the central focus of all her teachings.

The first six series of Bible Interpretations were presented at her seminary in Chicago, Illinois. The remaining Series', probably close to thirty, were printed in the Inter Ocean Newspaper in Chicago. Many of the lessons are no longer available for various reasons. It is the intention of WiseWoman Press to publish as many of these Bible Interpretations as possible. Our hope is that any missing lessons will be found or directed to us.

Finally, a very special acknowledgement goes to Rev Natalie Jean, who has worked diligently to retrieve several of Emma's lessons from the Library of Congress, as well as libraries in Chicago. Rev. Jean hand-typed many of the lessons she found on microfilm. Much of what she found is on her website, www.highwatch.net.

It is with a grateful heart that I am able to pass on these wonderful teachings. I have been studying dear Emma's works for fifteen years. I was introduced to her writings by my mentor and teacher, Rev. Marcia Sutton. I have been overjoyed with the results of delving deeply into these Truth Teachings.

In 2004, I wrote a Sacred Covenant entitled "Resurrecting Emma," and created a website, www.emmacurtishopkins.com. The result of creating this covenant and website has brought many of Emma's works into my hands and has deepened my faith in God. As a result of my love for these works, I was led to become a member of Wise-

Woman Press and to publish these wonderful teachings. God is Good.

My understanding of Truth from these divinely inspired teachings keeps bringing great Joy, Freedom, and Peace to my life.

Dear reader; It is with an open heart that I offer these works to you, and I know they will touch you as they have touched me. Together we are living in the Truth that God is truly present, and living for and through each of us.

The greatest Truth Emma presented to us is "My Good is my God, Omnipresent, Omnipotent and Omniscient."

Rev. Michael Terranova

WiseWoman Press

Vancouver, Washington, 2011

LESSON I

The First Adam

Genesis 1:26-31 Genesis 2:1-3

With today's lesson we begin a six years' course of scripture study. The purpose of the committee on lessons is to take us on a journey through the history of man from his fall to his redemption as related in the Christian Hebrew Bible.

We start out with Genesis first and second chapters. The first chapter tells of spiritual man. The second tells of material appearance. The third chapter admits that all things upon the earth were created invisibly before they exposed themselves physically. The second chapter shows itself to be the description of the symbolic and unreal because it presents man upside down from his first estate. As trees reflected in water show top downward so the lofty godliness of man and earth as first pronounced "good" by the almighty truth is pictured "fallen" when explained secondly from the physical-sense standpoint.

1

The physical senses are the obedient servants of the language of man. They are the folded leaves of a book. They are able to unroll and extend to the infinite stretches of observation of all things in creation. They show forth now as matter in all its forms. When we tell them to proceed further and see beyond what they now do we shall see further, and the sounds of the mornings on Polaris will be easy to hear.

There is a man now in Chicago, who has talked to his muscles till he has trained them to lift nearly a ton's weight. One muscle only remains obdurate, not yet yielding to his talking. When that succumbs he will lift the ton. Then who shall say that those muscles which are willing to respond so far may not respond farther? Who shall limit the strength of the man described in Genesis first? May he not come forth clearer and clearer as right language is used?

Language is Jehovah God. It is written, "The word was God." The first man spiritual can see all things. There is nothing can obstruct his views. He is "good" in every faculty. He can hear and touch everything. Within us is that "good" man with all his good facilities and good possessions. As it is written *"Christ in you."* (Colossians 1:27)

<u>Man the Image of Language.</u>

The man who has trained his muscles by talking to them shows the dominion language. Man is in the image and likeness of the language used to formulate him. It was once sacrilegious to think of the "six days" of creation as referring to periods of time. It expanded the thoughts of men when they alluded to vast extents of time and at once men were younger in feeling. It made all men younger at 60 than they had formerly been considered at 40. In Hamlet's address to his mother we would think she must be an aged fright, while from the customs of those times she must not be much past 30. Contemplation of vast and unnamed spaces of activities as forever unrolling has extended the youth of mankind. Who shall say that purer and truer contemplation may not expose the eternal youth of the "Elohim" — sons of God — ourselves? The language of truth is contemplation. "Have dominion over every living thing," says the God in man to all mankind. This lesson is a trumpet-call to notice how pure talking is the actual arising from beds of limitation to set forth into the open tells of freedom.

It is written. "Arise, let us go hence." On the strength of our pure and unafraid language we will arise from hindrances and go unhindered into the light.

There is one name of pure speech that is not much used. It is light. The city had no need of the sun, for God was its light. God is language. "Thy sun shall no more go down" when thy language never descends. Ruskin tells us that the sun is the power of man's arms and the sun is the power of his mind. Hear this: "Today, in the strength of your youth, you may know what it is to have the power of the sun taken out of your legs and arms. But when you are old, you will know what it is to have the power of the sun taken out of your mind also. Such a thing may happen to you sometimes, even now, but it will continually happen to you, when you are my age. You will no more, then, think over a matter to any good purpose after 12 o'clock in the day. *Sol illuminatis nostra est; Sol salus nostra; Sol sapientia nostra"* — Eagle's Nest, p.365.

Paul and Elymas

The sun of mind is Truth. The darkness of mind is the talk that hides truth. Paul struck Elymas blind by his condemnation of him for not being more and knowing more. Elymas represents money. Money represents obedience of things to thoughts. "I would be more and show you many places and give you many opportunities gladly," said Elymas. "You know nothing and you amount to almost nothing," said Paul. So Elymas groped in darkness. To your money you say, "You know nothing, and are altogether too little to show me the world to get me what I want." So your obedient money gropes around showing you none of its possibilities except as what you wish it might be. Why is this when you have dominion over the earth? Shall you not now seize upon your majesty and talk more -wisely to your Elymas?

The lame man at the beautiful gate represents mankind sitting in obstacle. "Peter and John in the firm and gracious words of Jehovah, "have dominion over every creeping thing." Our hopes and faith are able to dissolve every hindrance. They can fly on free wings of prosperity.

"We shall not fade nor fall,

While faith and hope prevail.

Think this moment of the most beautiful object your eyes ever beheld. Remember it for a brief space of time. Has not your mind sat at this gate looking at your poverty, or at your debt, or at your disease long enough so that you are willing to remember for a time the most beautiful object you ever beheld? Now let these two faces gaze into yours. First, "You are free." Second "Your own words are capable of making you equal with God himself." Look at them with the memory of that beautiful object in your mind. A miracle will be wrought on the line you are not expecting one. The lame man asked for gold and got strong feet. The prayer you have been praying is not answered by looking up to the sun-tipped cherubs on the gate at whose base your hindered feet ache. But something you have not asked to happen shall come to you.

Think, while you are awake early in the night watches of the most innocent face you ever beheld. Look at it as long as you can face it. This will take you back to the country of purity from whence you came forth. Elisha took the salt of innocence and healed the barren land and water where the theological school was established. They had been looking at sin. He turned their thoughts to innocence. *"The pure in heart see God."* (Matthew 5:8) This is rest. God is rest. "He rested." A new truth will arise with the innocent every morning.

Inter Ocean Newspaper, January 7, 1894

LESSON II

Adam's Sin and God's Grace

Genesis 3:1-15

The judgment day has arrived when all men have equally good judgment.

Why did God make Satan? He did not make him. He permitted him in order that there might be angels excelling in strength. There can be no victories without battles — Peloubet's Select Notes, p.20. (Annual Select Notes on the International Bible Lessons)

Where did God get Satan to permit? Let us have good judgment.

Jesus Christ called Satan a liar and the father of lies. Then if Satan says, "I am," he lies. If he says, "I was," he lies. If he says, "God permitted me," he lies, and whoever tells such stuff is like unto him. By this process of reasoning we are metaphysically free from Satan. That is we are mentally free. Tell a child there is an invisible Satan prowling around, and the child will some

7

day or night see some shape made visible which will be its formulated ideal of badness. (Vide Luther and the Wesleys.) The lie has passed from your mind to the child's mind and come out as a black man with horns.

Tell the child there is no Satan and there never was any, and the child will never see one. For mind never experiences anything it does not name. The eyes and nerves never feel anything their manager has not named and described.

"Charge some that they teach no other doctrine except of Jesus Christ", said Paul. (1 Timothy 1:3)

"Neither give heed to fables which minister questions rather than godly edifying." (I Timothy 1:4)

Fable of the Garden

If there ever was a fable that ministered questions to mankind it was that one about the good and Wise God's creating Satan and the primeval pair in Eden.

"The flesh profiteth nothing," said Jesus Christ. Why? Because all flesh is but the outward product of language.

This third chapter of Genesis, to which our attention is called, is a lesson in speech and its fruits. The Lord God is the law of the good as it affects matter and evil. While our language is occupied with good and evil there will always be the hope extended of a time when good is victorious. The Adam nature of man calls good evil and evil good. He complained of Eve, who was his gift of God. Eve complained of her own gift of reasoning whereby she should know that God was all and Satan was nothing.

In the fullness of time, her reasoning should break out as a science of God, which should bruise all evil out of the world. That time is now.

He who complains of his best friends is playing at Adams game. He is arranging arduous tasks for himself. He who complains of the reasoning faculty is playing at Eve's game. He is arranging great physical agony for himself. Look out for sickness.

Looked for Sympathy

Both Adam and Eve complain of not having enough and being enough. They thought they ought to be sympathized with. Whoever is looking for sympathy is playing at the game of Adam and Eve. Whoever sympathizes is playing at the serpent's game. But it is a fable from beginning to end because the pair that God made and pronounced "good" were incapable of actually experiencing the Adam and Eve nonsense.

There is a divine spark of lightning from the true God in every creature. It never gets entangled with the talk that formulates Satan, hard work, or sickness. It has been surrounded by this talk for ages, but never has paid any attention to it.

He who studies Adam, Eve, Satan, may get mixed into their quality if he likes and institute a manner of getting out of the maze. He may keep himself free from it if he pleases by knowing them as nothing at all.

He may think that some time they will be gone or he may think they will be eternal. "Matter is eternal," says one. "It is the shadow that is lost in spirit," says another.

"We shall have to throw away this pottage," said the students at Gilgal. But Elisha put meal into the pottage and it was healed of its poison.

"The time for the deliverance of man from the clutches of Adam is slow," say the people. But whoever knows there was no Adam and knows that the whole story is a fable is exempt now, to-day, from everything Adam and Satan are supposed to have blocked us into. The healing meal for the poison of time is one truth. Think it over carefully and see how quickly you will be set free. "Adam and Eve and Satan are the fable of the language of good and evil with reward and pun-ishments named instead of fruit of lips."

The True Doctrine

This is right doctrine. What is your judgment of it? What you think about it runs into it at right angles or diagonally at an acute angle and will strike fire. If it seems true and reasonable a strong demonstration will take place. An entirely new event will transpire which will please you greatly.

If you cannot accept it no such event will take hold of you.

To "eat of the fruits of the trees of the garden except one" is to know all about good and nothing about evil. Reasoning teaches that the word if evil will seem to fruit if the word of good is capable of fruiting. God the divine intelligence knows that neither good nor evil is reality.

Reasoning would keep mind harping on the law of cause and effect, both good and evil. God, the divine intelligence spark would have none of either cause or effect.

A contradiction of evil is as eye-opening as a contradiction of good. Disputing causes to look two ways at once. That true God is straight ahead.

The good always determines what is evil and what shall happen to evil. So God, the good, represented as showing Adam and Eve and the serpent what comes of their disputing the good. "To talk of evil is to die." "To talk of good is to live." But there is neither death nor life for the divine unquenchable lightning spark. It is exempt from such logical reasonings.

He who has, as Adam, got into the meshes of believing that hunger and poverty and sickness are real, will sit on the side of a good reasoning and praise of the good till he arrives into experiencing happiness. Then he will realize that happiness is real only just long enough to forget all misery. As it is prophesied: *"They shall forget misery."* (Proverbs 31:7) He will next call bliss as unreal as misery. He will then behold God. *"The pure in heart see God."* (Mathew 5:8) No happy man is pure enough to behold God, as no unhappy man is pure enough. The lightning spark is non-conformist.

It sees God without the pull of good and without the cramp of evil. It is God itself.

Concentrate all attention toward it and you see yourself as you are. In truth you are it.

Inter-Ocean Newspaper, January 14, 1894

LESSON III

Cain and Abel

Genesis 4:3-13

A Prussian physician discovered that there is a region within every man that is not sick, no matter how sick a man may seem to be. Religion is based on the discovery that there is a region within every man that is not sinful, no matter how contemptibly a man may perform.

Mocking is a great principle. It is sometimes spoken of as imitation. We certainly do grow to look and act like the people and conduct we observe around us. Then we radiate a quality about us, which other people and even objects assimilate.

The Shinto teachers tell their ministers never to look at their audiences in order that they may not be distracted from looking at their own thoughts. We are able to look at a thought as steadily as at a person. And afterward we as certainly appear and perform like that thought as we appear and perform like the people we look at.

13

The Prussian physician kept his eye on the region in his patients where they were wholesome. This restored them to health. Jesus kept his eye on the sinless region of those who followed him constantly, and this restored their whole character to nobility.

Some men keep their mind's eye perpetually on the poverty and mournfulness of this planet. Such men diffuse gloom and discouragement unconsciously. They are called philanthropists and reformers. Keep away from them. Keep them off your premises, unless you have the secret of Jesus concerning contagion. His secret was the art of keeping the mind's eye on the joyous and merry department within even the "reformers' mind.

"That thou seest

That thou beest."

This department is irresistibly contagious. It is omnipotent. It is perfection. It is the soul region. It is the God in man. Whoever talks about Adam and Eve and Cain is not looking at the soul region of the human race. Whoever talks about Jesus Christ is looking at the soul region of the human race.

Types of the Race

The book of Genesis exhibits all the regions of the race mind under the titles of Jubal, Tubal-Cain, Lamech, Abel, and so on. We are asked to notice such men today as are named in Genesis 4. Each one represents a streak in every man's make up as well as in the race mind *in toto*.

It is self-evident truth when we say "God is indestructible, unchangeable, spirit." It is reasonable to say: "The God in man is his undiscourageable, undefilable center." It is common sense to state that if there is such a region in each street-sweeper, it is wise to find out the method for exposing it. It is the province of science to proclaim that the Abel, Cain, Adah, Zillah regions, or streaks of man are not his indestructible and undiscourageable soul. They are "the shadow systems gathered round the me."

Therefore when I discuss Cain and Abel, I discuss shadows. If I get sorry for the murdered Abel or "righteously indignant" at Cain, who "slew him," I am wound up in shadows. If there is a science that can enable one to look at fools and thieves and know that they are not real and never were real, that must be the ethical science man is searching after.

The forty children of Bethel saw only the baldheadedness of Elisha. They mocked it. That is, they imitated his belief in old age and hugged them to death. God never has baldheadedness leading to decrepitude and the cemetery. The God region in Elisha was immortal youth and deathless strength. These young people should have been as careful to see the young and beautiful godhood of Elisha as the Prussian physician was to see the undefilable health of his patients.

God in the Murderer

The fourth Genesis causes a young man to ask many questions concerning God and man that his teachers are either obliged to hush him up or come right out with the truth of the case and call it a parable of the way thoughts act when men believe in the shadow system as a reality.

Where did Cain get his murdering ability? From Adam. Who was Adam? Nobody. Did not he ever live? No.

Have we not all an Adam nature, *"prone to err as the sparks to fly upward?"* (Job 5:7) No. How can you say that when appearances all show that way? So does the sun appear to rise in the east, but it does nothing of the kind. Don't you believe that any man ever murdered his fellow man? No. What were Guiteau and Prendergast? Nothing. How can you be so ridiculously foolish when our wisest scholars prove that they were criminally wicked people? Because, like the Prussian physician with his eye on the wholesome region, and like Jesus with his eye on the soul of the thief on the cross, I must keep my eye on the God in Guiteau and Prendergast. If I put my eye on the streaks they will increase. If I put my eye on the light, it will light the whole world. I must be "one pointed," as the Brahmins taught, or "single eyed" as Jesus taught. I must not mind what the masters and scholars upon the earth teach, for *"the Lord will cut off both the master and the scholar"* (Malachi 2:12) that give their mind up to the ac-

16

knowledging evil, while the "simplest man who in his integrity worships (or sees only) God," becomes God.

If I am to manifest what I see in you, I prefer to see God in you now and forever. Then Cain is only a myth. He is just a statement of how mixed up and unhappy a mind is that lets itself see itself as less wonderful than it is. As soon as you or I see ourselves as less wonderful, less capable, less beautiful than we are, we are Cain. It is a destructive sight. As soon as we admit that we are partly wise and partly foolish, sometimes good and sometimes bad, we are Abel. When our great men; so called, tell us that God has made some people to be beautiful and some to be ugly, some brilliant and some dull, they are Cain. When we agree with them, we are Abel. We get rubbed out with discouragement and they stay on *among men with their Tubal-Cains. "artificers in brass and iron" (Verse 22), and their Jubal-Cains, "musicians and philosophers."* (Verse 21)

God Nature Unalterable

We can play with our Cain and Abel myths for 6,000 years, if we like, but it will not defile or alter our God nature. But as 6,000 years of looking at unreality is quite long enough to play with shadows, we now rise in our Jesus Christ reality and proclaim that *God in man as all there is of man all there ever was of him, and all there ever will be of him.* (Genesis 1)

Within each living creature is "one who knows." That is the one who dares. It is that one who knows he cannot be slain, and he cannot slay. Shall I be interested in the foolish and cowardly while the steady glory of that everlasting nobility is shining on my face from the immortal heights of every creature's soul telling me "if I see it, I be it," and that is lofty wisdom to be it and the visibility of Jesus Christ to acknowledge it?

Whether this word reach the outer ears of the multitude or this doctrine strike their outer sight makes no difference. The mental breezes waft its saving truth into the universal heart, where judgment sits on, her eternal throne. It does not need recognition by external man; it is already being smiled upon by the true man of God dwelling in all men.

Inter-Ocean Newspaper January 21, 1894

LESSON IV

God's Covenant with Noah

Genesis 9:8-17

Myths and Bible stories depict the state of each man's mind under the dominion of some one or other idea. The Greek allegory of Amor and Psyche teaches the redemption of intuition from the emotions. The story of Elijah and Elisha teaches the effect of peaceableness set free from sternness.

Viewed in this way they all become excellent directions in the practice of what the theosophists call "Raja Yoga," or right handling of thoughts.

From Sankyha philosophy to astrologers' "charms," religion and ethics are struggling to instruct men how to attain beatitude, or exemption from every sort of ill. Religion seems to have "given up the ship" of expectation that exemption from misery is possible this side the tomb. The pulpit assures me that "man is born to trouble."

It is written of the worm that at the least pressure it turns. It is recorded of Mary that once she

19

did something on her own responsibility. She had always faithfully obeyed Martha till that day. It is told of Abel's blood that it is talking up its rights. It was not till Elijah was "cut off from the head" of obedient Elisha that Elisha fed a famished city, increased corn and loaves, raised the dead, watered thirsty armies, and defended himself from enemies by peaceful, peaceable, unrevengeful spiritual qualities, quite unlike his master's explanation of how miracles were wrought. The schools of Gilgal and Jericho understood that the reign of violence and vengefulness must give place eventually to spiritual mercifulness. The students of both schools told Elisha that, *"This day must thy master (Elijah), be cut from thy head."* (2 Kings 2:3) This is one of the very few 'instantaneous treatments" given in religious "Raja Yoga."

Jesus Christ gave one: *"Now is the accepted time."* (2 Corinthians 6:2) Millions of Christians have pounded on that treatment, denied it, explained it away, pointed to the state of the world and argued from hope, but here it is, just as simple, just as true as ever, "Now is the accepted time."

Value of Instantaneous Action

We have thousands of people striking and stamping theological proposition that "this day shall doing the work of the universe by stern effort be cut off from the head of church of the spirit, but here are the enemies of the globe standing still and the looms and traffic of creation idle because that treatment has gone forth with its irresistible demonstrableness. John Webster said: "Strike while the iron is hot."

Thousands, yea millions, have hurried and scurried to find the right instant to strike on their affairs to accomplish their purposes because his mind was strong and compelled them to think as he told them.

But there is another story to tell of the cold iron of your human lot as it enters into your heart today, the result of the strife and struggle of your past. You can strike that iron with the hammer of some simple truth it is white hot with joyousness.

Noah saw the rainbow setting its seven-hued arch against the cloud-curtained eastern sky. To all the inhabitants of his world it meant that a storm had come and gone, with death and terror on its wings, and might so come and go again. He set up his protest. He rose away from the man of affairs as the man of rest, and so spoke once from his own instinct. His name meant "rest." When he wrote with the pen of his own genius across the face of one item of nature's proud caravan, it responded with glad obedience. Noah's resurrection of his own native genius has testified that the rainbow stands an everlasting promise that the waters shall never cover the earth again but shall stay in their appointed basins till the heavens be dissolved and the mountains are no more.

The Lessons of the Rainbow

This is the lesson we are told in Genesis, 9:8-17. Noah rose from his hiding place. Rest rose from its brow-beaten darkness. Noah had obeyed struggle, effort, brave persistence. This was not his native talent. Drowning, crying, despairing were the fruits of rest being kept out of sight and struggle put foremost.

Within every mind is the Noah quality. If it is given freedom it marks every object with divine kindness. Nothing from thenceforth hath power to hurt. Leonardo da Vinci, sitting motionless before the altar cloth till his Noah quality was set free, painted something to the lasting story of the power of the spirit.

"In returning and rest shall ye be saved; in quietness and confidence shall be your strength." (Isaiah 30:15)

On the cold, hard want of this age there are some unnamed lovers of the doctrine of meekness, softly but commandingly printing a principle seven times heated with its own dissolving might. As the spirit of gentleness was Elisha's miracle worker, and it wrought no wonders for the world till the stern rigors of Elijah were taken away from mastership over him; as Noah's genius for command could only rise after the stormy terrors of cursing had had full sway, so not till the mind of man has ceased to look for prosperity by worldly struggle and competitions may the gentle doctrine of Jesus be seen as able by its own utterance to do all things that mind can ask.

There is no practice more successful than letting myself be myself, for at its edict it is meant that nature shall bend the knee. There is that within every man that is opposed to war and competition. It is the Noah quality. It is the stillness of the changeless divinity which in this lesson is called Noah talking with God.

When we hang on the dark skies of misfortune the true doctrine of Jesus, they shine with the promise that misfortune shall never deluge our mind and life forevermore.

"If a man keep my sayings he shall never see death," (John 8:51-52) of peace or joy. There is no handling of thoughts can equal these sayings. They undo the practices that have hitherto prevailed over man, subtly, noiselessly, easily. They usher in exemption from every ill. They make God visible.

Inter-Ocean Newspaper January 28, 1894

LESSON V

Beginning of the Hebrew Nation

Genesis 12:1- 9

Golden Text; "I will bless thee and make thy name great; and thou shalt be a blessing." (Verse 2)

Mozart said in his letters that whenever he saw a grand mountain or a wonderful piece of scenery it said to him, "Turn me into music; play me on the organ." So whenever one who is devoted to the mind principle reads the Bible stories he immediately sets the historic characters to some mental quality and reads the book of some man's fate backward and forward. He who has for his ruling mind trait the Abram quality will find himself moved up and away from his neighbors.

Was not Anaxagoras banished for teaching that there is one divine mind acting upon the universe with intelligence and design? "Abram" means "exalted father." Whoever has one high theme that occupies his mind as truth in the midst

24

of a society satisfied with lower themes will be assured by his own inner consciousness, or reassured by some unusual phenomenon formulated for his sake, that the lofty theme shall some day have a multitude of followers. *"And I will make of thee a great nation."* (Verse 2)

The Abram theme that is rising now in the mind of society as the founder of a universal nation is this: "There is only God." It is as ostracizing to you to hold this theme in your confidence today if you attempt to express it and specify as it was for Abram, B.C. 1921, to proclaim: "There is but one God." For society, judging after the sight of the eyes and the hearing of the ears, still holds, as Ur of old, that many principles rule our world besides changeless harmony. Some start up from the bottomless deeps of their imagination the proposition that there is disease occupying space and spot, and where he holds his red and black carnivals, there is no sign of the kindness of God. Some reel forth the fanciful yarn of a ruler called "want," whose reign it is the struggle of their life to undo. They cannot agree with what the Abram doctrine exalting itself in the mind of many Christians today. So the Christians' crowning glory, their noblest truth, the coming faith of the world, "departeth as the Lord commandeth" into the silent regions where the new people shall be born whose religion shall rule the earth.

No Use For Other Themes

When the Abram theme gets to ruling there is no use for any other theme to set up its claim. A man will keep silent if he believes God is all, but he will not descend to believe in anything else after he has felt the buoyant winds of that truth bearing him up on their pinions, thrilling him with their promises.

We read in Japanese religious myths what a clinch Bimbogami has on the actions of a man when he gets uppermost in his mind. Bimbogami means the idea of poverty. We have seen Bimbogami get uppermost as an idea in millions of minds. We see how destitution and despair show forth as the fruitage of the theme called poverty. But this lesson shows what follows, having for an uppermost theme: "There is but one." Jesus Christ said it was a prospering theme. "Ye shall have a hundred fold more in this life." It promised Abram "great name, great power, great blessings."

The theme, "There is only God," promises absolute immunity from hardship. It goes as an army of protection before the man who holds it. *"Be not afraid, I have overcome the world."* (John 16:33) It furnishes him his home and his comrades. *"I go to prepare a place for you."* (John 14:2) It goes as merciful motherhood. *"I will send the Comforter."* (John 14:16) It comes as wonderful wisdom, touching pen with subtle fires and tongue with irresistible lightnings. *"The Holy Ghost shall teach you all things."* (John 14:26)

It promises the ends of the earth for an audience. *"I am with you even to the end of the world."* (Matthew 28:20) It may look quite the contrary for many days and nights to the Abram quality of today when it sets up its rule. Poverty and deformity may set up their tabernacles on your premises if your heart has liberated the Abram doctrine of our age, *"but every knee shall bow and every tongue confess"* (Philippians 2:10-11) that it is the right doctrine.

Have you not read how the promise, *"I will make thy name great,"* (Genesis 12:2) was fulfilled so perfectly to Abram that no man has ever yet been so widely and so permanently honored, since both Mohammedans and Jews, equally with Christians, honor the name and character of Abraham? Have you not read how he was prosperous on every plane, fulfilling the decrees of right doctrine, that on no plane shall there be destitution when one gives it the ruling of his destiny?

Influence of Noble Themes

Do you suppose there are beggars in the kingdom where noble themes are regnant? Do you suppose there are crimes in the realm where the science of Christ is understood? Thus does one who perceives how it works with a man to give free reign to his most exalted theme call attention to the thinking principle. "If you can manage your draughts, your stove will broil and bake to perfection," says the stove man. "If you can manage your talking, your body will perform to perfection," says the man who, by talking to his body, gets it to performing great feats. "If you can handle your thoughts, you can fill the convolutions of your brain with sparkling globules of that gray matter so beloved by great thinkers," says the thought wind as it blows past our heads, entering only where our mind doors are open. "If you will let an exalted theme be your only theme, it will lift you out of the depths; it will buoy you over the breakers; it will waft you on wings of glory; God shall wipe away your tears; angels shall feed and clothe you; Jesus Christ will work miracles for you wherever you walk." There is only God to him who knows it is true that there is only God.

Abram should not have "taken Lot along with him" till he had transmuted Lot's quality from clouding and covering his face all the time with inability to see how an exalted principle works. Abram's blind obedience was like the cook's blind obedience to the stove man's directions about draughts. It is possible to see into the principle of draughts. It is possible to see an idea in its workshop. But even those who believe there is only God are lugging along a "Lot" who keeps them from seeing clearly what manner of movements their high truth loves best and keeps them from seeing where their noble truth will fulfill itself.

Danger In Looking Back

The "Lot" which the Abram doctrine is now covered with is the teaching that "there is no God," without the potency within itself to make itself consistent with "there is only God," without a great deal of controversy. It causes its hearers to look back to doctrines exposed on less giddy heights. But having taken these two friendly propositions, none can "look back" without being petrified as Lot's wife.

"Sarah" is the only companion "Abram need take," which means that whoever holds the principle clearly that there is only God, will have the name "Jesus Christ" woven into it and with it till its hidden potency shall break forth. *"I know thy works, and where thou dwellest, and thou holdest fast my name,"* (Revelation 2:13) and *"I will give thee a white stone, and in the stone a new name."* (Revelation 2:17) *"And the Lord said unto Abram, Unto thy seed will I give this land."* (Verse 7) The name that accompanies the "exalted father" is "Prince of Peace," as Sarai was Princess of the Home. Having them in thy heart, "there shall no ill come nigh thy dwellings."

"And Abram journeyed, going on still toward the south." (Verse 9) "The south" is a figure of speech for warmth, gladness, harmony, beauty, wisdom. Those who have the one and only regnant principle of today already can sight the white promontories of New Canaan's happy shores.

Inter-Ocean Newspaper February 4, 1894

LESSON VI

God's Covenant With Abram

Genesis 17: 1-9

Two angels accompany every one of us from al-
pha to omega. Their names are Peace and
Happiness. One is never realized without the
presence of the other. These two angels are to the
mind what the eyes are to the head, for they behold what lies before and show what is the right
path. It is written of little children that "their angels do always behold the face of the father." The
father is God. When the child looks into its mother's face it sees only God. When it no longer sees
God in its mother's face, it is no longer a child.

When a child feels the sunshine of God's face
hot and wonderful, we remark of it that it is a
genius. Every genius had once some way of being
happy and peaceful long enough to feel the sunshine of the face of God on its face. Thus,
Paganini, while yet a boy, astonished Italy with
his music. Thus, the Genoese traveler and his
genius for discovering new lands pushed him out

over stormy waters safely to the yellow sands of the free new West.

Humboldt wrote in the register of a mountain hotel, "Citizen of the World." Jesus Christ wrote on the pages of the summit wisdom of all time, "Citizen of Heaven." He had a genius for finding heavenly places and seeing heavenly sights everywhere. The cripple never looked crippled to him. He saw in his face the face of God, and saith unto him, "One is your Father." The sinner never looked sinful, the leper was not repulsive, the prisoner was forever free in his eyes. "The kingdom of God is within you."

As Little Children

Is it possible, after having seen sinners and beggars, to return again into a childhood's vision which sees only God? We are under orders to "become as little children." Abram had an "H" from Jehovah's own name, and Sarai also received the mark of the child in her forehead and became Sarah. The disciples of Jesus became wise in discovering the perfections of man. Wherever their eyes fell on people and things, they showed forth their godhood.

People who abide in peace accomplish more miracles than the strivers and strainers. *"Abram believed in the Lord, and it was accounted to him for righteousness!"* (Genesis 15:6) "The Lord" is the self of man. The more a man believes in himself the more good he sheds abroad. He often looks through peace and happiness into the face of God.

He makes no effort to convert the heathen when he sees the goodness and holiness of the Father in their faces.

It is possible to be such a genius at sighting goodness and wisdom in the faces of men that it would be accounted a subtle species of stealing on my part if I were to aver that any one of them was a heathen or reprobate. It is possible to be such a genius at sighting the knowledge of God in man's hearts that it would be accounted a species of stealing on my part if I were to proclaim that they ought to have missionaries to teach them God.

"He who filches from me my good name

Doth that which not enriches him nor any man."

If every man on the earth would often tell what he honestly believed in his own self, he would soon begin to show forth his innate greatness. Does he verily believe in his own integrity? Let him tell himself this truth often within his own soul. Does he believe in his own ability? Let him acknowledge it in so many words to himself. Does he believe that he is in the right in that which he calls his religion? Let him affirm that he is in the right.

God and Mammon

No man ever felt any soul rest except in what he honestly believed himself to be. This is called his own "bed" in our Bible. *"Take up thy bed and go thy way."* (Matthew 9:6) The time when one takes an honest survey of what he does believe, is after he has been struggling on some line, which has not accomplished anything. Do you believe that God clothes you, or do you believe that money clothes you? Could you travel from Chicago to New York without money? Could you have a mouthful to eat without money? What are you working for? Do you wonder that some people have affirmed that money is God?

As a people making money our god, we have reached our bitter extremity. Of such it is written, *"The prayer of faith shall save, and God shall raise him up at the last day."* (John 6:4) "Abram was ninety and nine," (Verse 1) and no signs of a son through whom to propagate himself had been given. Then he made a new covenant. As our world has arrived at its 99th percent of trouble, let it now, before it tastes its 100th percent thereof — which is starvation, make its covenant with its God. When a man tells what he believes, he is making a covenant with a principle. The principle he tells himself he honestly believes in is the one that will work with him. *"I am Almighty God. Walk before me and be thou perfect."* (Verse 1)

If, when you tell what you honestly believe, you feel happiness and peace in any degree, you are then beholding the face of God, and it will surely be a "treatment" which will stimulate your native genius. Your own greatness will come forward. As you are truly greater than circumstances and environments, no matter how powerful they may seem to be, it is right for you to know it. To

34

Abram, 1,900 years before Jesus, his own worthiness was so real to him that it spoke audibly.

Being Honest With Self

His own greatness, goodness, worthiness was his God. If money is your God it will do you good to acknowledge it to yourself and talk to your money face to face. The main proposition of today's lesson is: Be honest with yourself as to what you believe is good in yourself and what you believe it is good for you to have. This honesty will begin a new base for you to operate upon. A new base is an excellent thing. Taken after the order and direction of this lesson, thou mayest be confident that *"kings shall come out of thee."* (Verse 6)

The people have been slyly believing in money as their dependence, but outwardly proclaiming God the invisible spirit as their support. This has made a slimy basis. Now they face themselves up and begin again. This is strength, discovery of new powers, inspiration. And in our chapter now before us, inspiration and greatness are called "kings."

When a pietist after the Guyon, Fenelon type of abusing his body, calling himself a monkey, reviling the world, calling it a snare and wickedness, faces himself up he will ask, "Why am I teaching myself to hate the outer world and my body, whose house of abiding I find myself in? Within me do I hate or love them?" He will say, "I love them. I believe they are beautiful and comfortable till I abuse them and revile them. The people are lovely to me till I strike them with the lash of my will-trained tongue."

Immediately, the pietist will begin a new base. This will be "a new covenant."

It is the exquisite honesty of the child that makes it so free, so wise, so beautiful. It is its honesty that causes its two angels to face the true God and illuminate it with genius. He who is honest with himself, telling what quality he believes he has and what he believes is good for him to have, starts as a little child. Thus, Isaac was promised to Abram.

When we have practiced telling ourselves what we do believe, we shall find certain results have started themselves going in our character. These are called "generations" in the 9th verse. By "generations," we always understand the Bible to signify "results." Theosophists call results by the title "karma."

In pure character lessons, as related to environments, which is our ministry, we see the "results" of taking up our "bed" or faith, or making a new base, which is making a covenant, which is confessing our honest confidence.

Let us mention some character "generations" which Abram saw would be "everlasting possessions" to us.

   a) We shall be exactly what we pretend to be;

36

b) We shall be controllers of matter, not controlled by it;

c) No physical conditions can disturb the equilibrium of our mind;

d) We shall not need the favor of anybody to make us happy; we shall be above craving for love, sympathy or praise;

e) We shall appreciate our own unchanging divinity.

Inter-Ocean Newspaper February 11, 1894

LESSON VII

God's Judgment of Sodom

Genesis 18:22-33

There is a saying ascribed to Matthias (that apostle who took the place of Judas and was martyred in Ethiopia) which reads, "If the neighbor of an elect man sin, the elect man sinned himself."

There is a saying of Jesus, which reads, *"The kingdom of heaven (within you) is like unto leaven."* (Matthew 13:33) Said Alexander Dumas, "When man is no longer afraid of death for himself and no longer causes the death of his neighbor, then man is God."

Abraham, in this 18th Chapter of Genesis is practicing concentration of mind upon the power of righteousness. He fastens his mental gaze upon Sodom and struggles to see the ability of a less and less quantity of leaven to leaven the whole lump thereof. He sees that the least number of men agreeing upon one principle that can cause a large city to agree with them is ten.

The recognition of the right of all men to equal freedom from bondage of any kind, if held firmly by ten men in a city, causes all that city to recognize the right.

The recognition of the spiritual substance moving in all men, if held steadfastly by ten men in a city, will make all that city finally acknowledge that one force alone animates them, and that is Spirit.

Pantalaji, the Hindu sage, said: "By concentrating the mind upon minute, concealed or distant objects in every department of nature, one may acquire thorough knowledge concerning them."

The soul, the spirit, the divine spark, may seem minute, concealed, distant, in our neighbor, but if by concentrating our mind upon it we may cause it to stand forth, is it not worth practicing concentration to accomplish?

Abraham drew forth one man whom the intrepid Peter pronounces "righteous," although history describes him as the reverse. He had not the strength of gaze to see ten men, all of like mind with himself. The city looked too dark with sinfulness, but his faithful effort accomplished better than he planned.

The White Cross Legion had a motto, which was significant of the leavening power of mind focused to one pure principle, "My strength is as the strength of ten, because my heart is pure." It

has had a wonderful influence on public senti-
ment. The best motives of tens of thousands of
men have stood forth, and the baser have been
forgotten, as Lot was all that was left of Sodom.

No Right Nor Wrong In Truth

Take the Bible stories as personifying mind,
moral quality, and abstract principles. Abraham is
mind closing round the noble truth that God is all.
The statement is new, and all appearances of nature and human kind dispute it. While it is yet a
new statement, and Sodom has not yet been per-
meated with it, that other truth is made apparent,
viz., that there is in truth neither right nor wrong.
In truth, there are no descriptions of opposites.

Abraham willingly saw Lot as the only righteous man in Sodom. So if I feel secure and strong
in the might of my wonderful principle that God is
all there is, I become fearless to say that as my
idea of God has been my God, I am glad to let go
all my ideas for truth itself to have free transit
through me. Now it is plain that the world which
feels so divided between fear of virtue and fear of
vice can only be rid of its double fear by my saying
into its face that, in the spirit of the universe,
there is no virtue for the viceful to fear and no vice
for the virtuous to fear.

Thus Lot stands forth, who seems to darken
and to hide the glory of the young recognition that
God is all, filling the sands with his substance,
and the scorpions with his goodness. For Lot is
utterly indifferent to virtue and vice, pain and

peace, right and wrong. He does not claim to be righteous or wicked. He is an impersonal, unformulated statement of the principle, willing to be the skill of the forger and of the detective, praised by Peter, scolded by Calvin, raining on the just and on the unjust alike, drowning the mission ship "Morning Star" and the pirate boat all in one breath by their both alike believing in Satan and Jesus: one fearing Jesus, the other fearing Satan.

Shall not the fear principle operate according to its own regular method? And is it any wonder that mankind finds Lot a mysterious character? And is it not plain that the truth that now flows so freely through the channels made by the glorified First Principle is a mystery to all but those who are as open for abstract truth to flow unhindered by their preconceived ideas as Abraham? What a mystery is the truth that there is neither right nor wrong in truth!

Among the sayings of Jesus in common use among the primitive Christians was this: "Beholding one working on the Sabbath, he saith unto him, "Man, if thou knowest what thou doest, blessed art thou; but if thou knowest not, accursed art thou, and a transgressor of the law."

Ezekiel, prophesying of this doctrine when it should spring forth in these days as a mental science, wrote: "I will cut off from thee the *righteous and the wicked, saith the Lord.*" (Ezekiel 21:3)

Misery Shall Cease

There is no thought we can let stream through us more dematerializing than the Lot thought. And it is the explanation of all Sodom or all this planet. Principle is principle. Attend unto it and agree with it, that there shall be no pain and the very knowledge of pain may leave the planet. Attend unto it and agree with its almightiness, that misery shall cease. Attend unto it and agree with it, that happiness and ease shall not be purchased at the expense of the animals, of the poor, of the helpless.

"He will deliver the needy when he crieth, the poor also, and him that hath no helper."

Goodness that mourns over vice is not goodness. It is double sight. Jesus taught the advantage of single sight. *"Shall not the judge of all the earth do right?"* (Verse 25) asked Abraham. Whatever state of body, mind, surroundings we are now in, this is our judgment. Do not the lines and colors tell the age of a man?

"In whatsoever state I find you, in that I judge you," is now an acknowledged teaching of Jesus. This is right. This is leprosy, beauty, lameness, litheness. This is "karma." What doeth Jesus therewith? Standing in the door of Peter's house, "he suffered not these things to speak," the devils our visions call the karma, which we do not like.

There is nothing so understanding to the institutions of men as the two secret doctrines clearly

understood by the Jesus Christ in all men. Do you
understand how a man by knowledge could break
the Sabbath and not break it? Then you see how
Lot could talk and act as he did and purposely be
hastening the disappearance of Sodom, as the
wisest answer to Abraham's prayers. Abraham
found not ten to say, "The God in man is all there
is of man." Before he had drawn them out of the
shadows by concentrated intention, he saw that
his first idea of righteousness was fear and recognition of vice in a subtle form.

The whole city was saved when the mysterious
Lot was saved. Fear was burned as chaff. Who
built our magnificent churches? Men who feared
poverty, hunger, cold, debt. Who built our stately
prisons? Men who feared vice, death, pain. What
are they all, the cloud-capp'd towers, the solemn
temples, the great globe itself?" Sodom the double
fear. What shall become of them? Like Sodom,
"they shall dissolve, and like its insubstantial pag-
eant, faded, leave not a rack behind." What shall
be seen here where the shades of fear are settled
on our dear little earth with its little handful of
mankind? The countless Elohim who say, "there is
only God"; the angelic hosts who know neither
good nor evil; "the church of Pergamos which held
fast my name" till its new name, not citadel of
safety, but neither safety nor danger, was written.
*"Behold, I create new heavens and a new earth;
and the former shall not be remembered, nor come*

into mind." (Isaiah 65:17) Here are the Abraham, Lot, Sarah, Isaac, of the universal mind.

Inter-Ocean Newspaper February 18, 1894

LESSON VIII

Trial of Abraham's Faith

Genesis 22:1-13

When a man is bound to some old trait of character or prejudice which keeps coming up and interfering with his later principles, we say he is Ixion bound to his wheel. Abraham had been brought up to believe in slaughtering animals to appease the wrath of his God. He had often seen children sacrificed to suit the savage appetites of a watchful and jealous deity. Even after the gleaming majesty of his true relations with the real God had been vouchsafed, he clung to the notion of sacrificing something to curry further patronage from his Jehovah.

So much for simple history on the phenomenal plane of man's early struggles to lift himself from the hypnotism of church, state and school errors. Poor Abraham never unglued himself from the error of cutting up little lambs and calves to gratify the Almighty, and to this day certain of us are still psychologized by the ancient belief that our own life and health are prolonged and improved by stockyard tragedies. Only the supermost idealism, persistently preached till the songs of all the angels on all the Moriahs of all men's hearts are the only sounds heard, can hush the error that —

"Life ever more is fed by death,

In earth and sea and sky,

And that a rose may breathe its breath

Something must die."

While the question stirs the heart of man why such things should be, there will forever be the voice from the ideal, which is forever the only real, that "I will have mercy, and not sacrifice," "He that killeth an ox is as if he slew a man," and "Lay not thine hand upon the Lord's anointed."

We are not expected, according to the Jesus Christ doctrine, to look to these texts of Genesis from the materialistic standpoint. We need not trace the history of man's slow awakening from the ages old hypnotic stupor of that first suggestion to him of how the universe would look and act if God were not God and the God in man were not all there is of man.

Light Comes With Preaching

We hear the orders of the merciful and mighty Jesus Christ, *"What is preached to you in darkness (parables and Old Testament stories, which are symbols) that preach ye in the light"* (Luke 12:3) — which is that there is a real world standing in the midst of all that we are now looking at, and it shall appear in all the splendor of its light by our persistent talk and thought about it.

> *"We feel its airs blow o'er us,*
>
> *And a glory shines before us,*
>
> *Of how 'twas meant to be*
>
> *With all mankind."*

We sometimes hear men of great love and knowledge say that it is not much use to try spiritualizing the race by preaching to grownup men and women. They feel that our only hope is with the children. But they are talking from their sight of darkness. "Preach ye in the light!" commands Jesus Christ.

A horde of men came into the presence of Jesus Christ with a dark claim against a woman, chaining her by their agreement with sin. He said that there should be one without sin to first cast a stone at her. So he himself, the man entirely without sin, did cast a stone at her.

This was the stone he threw: "I see God in you." And all those men who stood for darkness sank into the sands as the light of the world rose on the doctrine of the reality of sin. *"Hath no man condemned thee?"* (John 8:10) he asked of the spotless soul. And the answer of the woman falls like an angel's harp into the fingers of the virgin mother of the coming race: *"No man, Lord."* (John 8:11) And he saith unto her: *"Neither do I condemn thee."* (John 8:11)

So the hardened men and women of the world have their uncondemned region, and he who would be the Jesus Christ to a world must see only that region in all the race, children and adults, animals and towering intellects in equal presence.

He who takes the stand that the spotless uncondemned soul of man is all there is of man is Abraham. He who takes this stand has joy born into him and forth from him. This is Isaac. He who still clings to his timorousness, to his first teachings of a personal God demanding more and more effort on his already overstrained life, is Abraham, thinking he must not expect joy yet awhile.

You Can Be Happy NOW

If you feel that you must wait a single minute for your joy, while yet you believe that the idea is the real, you are on Moriah. If you let the voice of your soul sing from its hidden heights on the Jesus Christ doctrine of "Now," you will be happy now. If you still think that though you are happy within your own soul and many blessings are yours, while your neighbors still dwell in ignorance and pain, which you cannot ameliorate, you are sacrificing lambs like Abraham.

Your neighbors are as much in the light as you are yourself. Your neighbors have their communions with their own white godhead as much and as often as you do. You shall not seize them from their free grass plots to bleat with pain on your altar of imagining that God is partial to you, and empowers you to call them unhappy and ignorant.

This is the translation of light on the 22nd of Genesis. The only sacrifice ever sung of in the celestial kingdom here abiding is that song of letting be the un-condemned spirit. Go not forth in mind with a knife to slay ignorance or sin. The only knife is the immortal truth that there is only one reality and it never heard of sin. Expect no provisions of food or instruction for the race, for in soul where the race now dwells, they know no want and they gleam and glow with the wisdom they had in the beginning and which can never be taken away. If this be transcendentalism, then Jesus Christ was a transcendentalist, for this is His doctrine.

Inter-Ocean Newspaper February 25, 1894

LESSON IX

Selling the Birthright

Genesis 25:27-34

The subject of this lesson is "Appetite." Esau was hungry for physical food. Jacob "was hungry for honors.." "Isaac loved Esau because he did eat." "Rebekah loved Jacob" for the same reason.

When a man is hungry for knowledge and ignores his bodily appetites, he speaks slightingly of the Esau type whose eyes glisten as he describes game dinners. When a man loves venison and tripe, he has not a voracious appetite for seeing all living things free and happy. He despises such sentimentality.

Protoplasm is the formless life stuff out of which all things are formed. Socrates or the red ant rears his head hungry from the start to eat up all the other amoebae. Protoplasm is filled with mouths. It is maw. It is the bottomless pit. Each mouth is an amoeba. Let not him that is hungry for the praise of men think himself any better off than he who is hungry for "lentil soup" or pate de fois gras. If he tries to convert his neighbors to his kind of appetite he is only an amoeba trying to swallow his neighbor amoeba.

Let not him who is hungry for information concerning the other world that lies so close to this that the rustling wings of its inhabitants may be heard at midnight, imagine that his appetite is a flick more Godlike than the reformer's hunger to find another den of infamy to groan about.

For God is not hungry for information; neither is He hungry to reform the wicked. God is satisfied. Thus he who has least appetite is nearest Godlike.

The struggle of the amoeba, whether his name be Plato or flea, for food to satisfy himself, is the struggle of all things to be satisfied with fullness as God is now satisfied. *"With thee is fullness of joy."* (Psalms 16:11) Nobody ever had enough to eat of the kind of food he had opened his mouth for. Is the richest woman in the world satisfied with the amount of money she has collected?

"Ye Shall Be Filled"

Did not Esau rest a little and then rise up with an increased stomach capacity? One would think that the man who "holds by universal consent the highest rank among the national philosophers of ancient and modern times," the author of the Principia might have felt some little sense of satisfaction, but no! Listen to his Oliver Twist-like cry for more: "To myself I seem to have been only like a boy playing on the seashore, whilst the great ocean of truth lay all undiscovered before me." Did you ever know of one who had praise enough to please him?

Jesus Christ taught that only one hunger would ever be satisfied. *"Blessed are they that do hunger and thirst after righteousness, for they shall be filled."* (Matthew 5:6) Righteousness means God, the one Spirit. There is an ability in the one Spirit filling heaven and earth with itself to satisfy all creatures who open their mouths with intention to swallow the whole spirit of God. "The Father and I will come and make our abode in you." Then ye shall be filled.

It is easy enough to say that Jacob was mean to take advantage of Esau's hunger to steal his birthright. It is easy enough to say that Jacob showed a lack of trust in the promises of God that he should have the birthright without trickery. It is easy enough to point out Esau's faults. For 3,700 years, historians and moralizers have been clear on the right and wrong of Jacob and Esau.

Let us look at the subject from a less hackneyed premise. When we read of *"Esau despising his birthright"* (Verse 34), we are reading of ourselves ignoring or turning away from some suggestion that is offered to us by a spoken word or secret principle. It is suggested to me that if I know the higher mathematics better than any living being, I shall have all the eyes of all the learning of Christendom turned toward me with admiring wonder. But I don't allow that amoeba in the protoplasmic ocean of void in which suggestions rear their hungry heads to eat me up. I, like Esau, exclaim, *"What profit shall this be to me?"* (Verse 32) I hand over to the Newtons of this age all my ambitions in this line.

So Newton despised me for having no appetite for trigonometry and I despised Newton for having no appetite for seeing all the world healed and transfigured. We are only repeating the Esau-Jacob serio-comedy.

It is all a matter of appetite, you on your hungry ethical plane, I on my hungry bodily plane; he on his hungry-for-money plane, she on her hungry-for-praise plane.

While the everlasting truth abides that God is hungry for nothing. How still the eternal God remains in the presence of folly. How silent the wonderful God keeps in the midst of this ceaseless eating!

The Delusion Destroyed

"O thou unshaken one! By thy favor my delusion is destroyed." For I see that it is all delusion, this chasing around after suggestions to eat, this conniving and twisting to keep from being worsted in the battle for existence. The unshaken one, the satisfied one, says one thing to the gnawing void: *"Look unto me and live."* (Isaiah 45:22)

"With heart that abides in me alone and to nothing else wanders, he, through meditation on the Divine Spirit, goes to it." He who goes to God is filled with God. He is filled. For God is able to fill even the soul.

There is one impartial Will that liveth and dieth not, and in that Will all that which ought to be is. When one is looking without himself to quench his thirst and supply his hunger, he is trying to look without to find God. And if he names the substance he is feeling around after by its right name, he will begin to be better fed. He will say, *"Thy will be done."* (Matthew 26:39)

If one is looking within himself to find the wherewithal to satisfy his appetite, and names what he is searching after by its right name, he will begin to be happier. He will say, "Thy will be done."

For in the impartial Will within me and in the impartial Will without me, which is the One Will, all that which ought to be is, and with that which is I am satisfied.

Ages of ages of naming the things without me and within me by the Adam suggestions of good and evil leave me still hungry.

Ages of naming the beauties and glories of heaven by the Joshua suggestions leave me still hungry. But one point of time shorter than the fraction of a second of sight and taste of the will of the Impartial One makes me God. I am awake and am satisfied.

The Adam man names both good and evil. The Joshua man names only good. He complains against nothing. The Jesus Christ man names neither good nor evil. He eats the Impartial Will, and is that Will. It makes its abode in him. We are like what we eat, on whatever plane we are feeding ourselves — Gentile, if Gentiles; moral, if morals; God, if God.

Inter-Ocean Newspaper March 4, 1894

LESSON X

Jacob at Bethel

Genesis 28:10-22

"Truth is thy star of destiny,

And if thou hast truth enough

To render thee a lofty-thoughted, honest man,

Thou hast enough to command The light of ages,

The influence of armies, The fate of empires.

Nothing shall to thee too early come,

 Nothing too late;

God is thy fate."

David wrote: *"In thy majesty ride prosperously because of truth."* (Psalms 45:4) But we must not imagine that anything whatsoever that we know of matter is truth. We have many statements concerning matter, but no one has looked majestic or felt majestic because of them. On the contrary, the student of insects who is quoted as authority on antennae invariably gets to looking like the coleoptera he knows most about. Chicago's specialist on carbuncles died of a most revolting one. You may count upon being bone of bone and sinew of sinew of what you are giving your attention unto. You look and act exactly like it.

All the health you have, all the nobility you have, all the intelligence you have, is what you believe of truth. If you have a bad disposition, are quick tempered, arbitrary, selfish, stingy, deceitful, it will not count anything against you if you are positive that one single beautiful proposition you ever heard concerning God is true and have paid good attention to it. That one statement is equal to defrauding your disposition of its prey at the very moment when the moral law would carefully explain you ought to be receiving its consequences.

Many Who Act Like Jacob

There is a large body of people now who would be beggars and sick if they had their desserts, according to the moral law. They have performed with their neighbors and brethren exactly like Jacob performed with Esau. But they have said with great confidence that God fills heaven and earth with his own substance, and there is none other substance anywhere. This mystic principle has worked through their environments like leaven. Today they are buoyed up and mysteriously provided for.

Jacob had one truth with which his destiny was wrought out to some measure of nobility and upon which he rode somewhat prosperously. It was this: "The Lord God brought it to me."

Even when he was stealing his father's blessing, he boldly insisted concerning the little kids which he had just killed, that the Lord God brought them to him to serve unto his father a savory dinner.

Truth is a well of water springing up. It is the Beersheba spot in each man's mind. Jacob lived with Isaac at Beersheba. He had a sneak-thief disposition, which ran him into dark hours, but he had truth enough to revive and cheer him every time. "Man's extremity is God's opportunity." "God is truth."

Jacob had not paid attention enough to his one truth to make him honest and lofty-minded every moment. One ought to notice the absolute truth continually if he would be so noble-thoughted and sincere that all knowledge, all influence, all fate, should be his own without any dark hours or sandy spots.

How to Seek Inspiration

There's many a theory concerning the stones, but there's no inspiration in stones as stones. Inspiration is in the well in the heart of the stone. If you are searching after knowledge you must search into the "ego" of the stone, or into its "well." The trees that lie softly on yon horizon beds of misty sky have somewhat wherewith to revive your drooping hours besides acorns and apples. If you are wise in trees, but do not know their reviving songs, you have wandered into "Haran," and are growing old and stiff like their shaggy barks. If you know their mystic wells and how to drink therefrom, you ride majestically on their buoyant qualities.

The story of Jacob is always the story of the church as it has performed and does perform and ever will perform till it proclaims where Jesus Christ, the living inspiration of the Almighty, truly is.

Has not the church a habit of hiring its pulpit to give it great nobility among the inhabitants of earth? When the church buys the minister's services, the church is buying Esau's birthright of free speech. The pulpit orator has always been "Esau." The church has always been "Jacob." We all know right well that "Esau" (that is, the minister) has to preach exactly what his audiences like, regardless of whether it is true or not, else he and his family may go hungry. So "Esau," who cannot bear to go hungry, whose heart would faint to see his children on the street, sells his birthright of free speech, and Jacob (the church) wanders to this day in "Haran" (which means "dry"). It is from the congregation (which is the "Jacob" of the church) that all privilege to express new ideas springs. Then as the church gives its gold and silver and good shelter (lentil soup) to its "Esau" in exchange for what the preacher really does believe, Jacob, the congregation, will have spells of seeing "angels," of hearing "promises," and trying to bargain with the very Lord Jehovah himself to take care of their prosperity if they "*will give one-tenth thereof to him.*" (Verse 22)

When Esau gives all his birthright freely forth, Jacob will not attempt to force the everlasting God down to accepting one-tenth of his earnings, one-tenth of his time, one-tenth of his heart.

Christ, the True Pulpit Orator

Jesus Christ was the genuine pulpit orator. He gave forth from the well within him regardless of whether the congregations furnished him with sandals or not. He taught plainly that his church must give all it had — all it had, each member of it — all its time to studying God; all its attention to watching God; all its heart to God. Nothing was said by him about selling pews to help pay for his dinners, nothing deferential in him to the man who put in one-tenth; he rather spoke boldly that the woman who put in all she had was drinking of the well he was drinking from, though she put in only one-fifth of a cent.

If you have truth enough to cause you to give your palatial doors wide swing for one to stand within your walls, and tell those men out there on your sidewalks that they are full of the God inspiration and may have their provisions straight from God by laying hold of the all-providing Spirit, and that by so doing they will find their sidewalks swept and garnished by miraculous winds, you have enough truth to make you bold.

The lily toils not, but its work is perfect. Jesus Christ toiled not, but his work rides majestically prosperous over the crumbled walls of ancient Rome, whose architects are forgotten. Had the Romans thrown over building temples and watched the wonderful one Spirit that Jesus was watching, their work too would be alive today.

There is one source of knowledge. There is but one knowledge. That is God. We need not be afraid our debts will not be paid if we are laying hold upon the owner of the stars. We need not fear that our children will go hungry if we are telling what we know is true of the here-present Jehovah.

It is not what we know of stones as stones that will give us support. It is what we know of the God inside and outside the stones that will feed us. While the world has been working with things as things, torturing matter for its knowledge, it has been in "Haran," the dry place. It has had angels, namely, great moments of inspiration, which have come down with sudden miracles of help in times of panting anxiety. It has put up noble statements from its soul center toward the heights. These also are angels.

Angels of ascending are proclamations of truth that work with the One Spirit. Angels of descending are the results of those proclamations. While we are in dry places, hungry, tired, anxious, we see our past few great thoughts going up to bring down help. But what if we had had only true thoughts every moment?

The Priceless Knowledge of God

Can I know anything worth knowing except God? While I am studying or working at anything else I shall wait and faint on the plains of effort, effort, effort. The primeval man pounded his nut against a stone till he wore his heart and hopes out, but still was struggling to get the meat. Then an angel turned his hand over and he pounded the stone on the nut and was fed. He who studies less than the One Spirit is pounding his nuts on stones.

How hard it has been for Jacob, the congregation of the church, to get his living by killing animals regardless of their shrieks, killing men on battle fields, employing little children, manufacturing merchandise! A fortune today, the poorhouse tomorrow, starvation in that garret, Crimean dainties in that palace — this is pounding nuts on stones. But lift up your heads, ye sons of men! God's presence bright is never absent. Truth on rounds of glory ascendeth now from the hearts of certain among us who, by attending unto God alone, find the promises of Jesus Christ really true. Take no thought saying, how shall we be provided for in this desert place, for your heavenly Father careth for you? *"Not by might nor by power, but by my spirit, saith the Lord."* (Zechariah 4:6)

Jacob need not have been in Haran the dry time. We need not have been in desolation. The church need not now be finding herself incompetent to help the shrieking throngs. But being in

Haran, lo! that which Jacob said, "The Lord gave me the kids," having also been said by us, now brings down its blessings. In such an hour as we think not to be helped, God shall swing the true things he once spoke of himself down to our protection and providing and strengthening.

> *"If thou hast spoken truth enough*
>
> *To hold thy thoughts aloft always,*
>
> *Thy light shall always shine,*
>
> *Thy strength shall never fail,*
>
> *Thou art not less than God himself."*

Inter-Ocean Newspaper March 11, 1894

LESSON XI

Jacob's Prevailing Prayer

Genesis 32:9-12 Genesis 24:30

The subject of this lesson is "Prevailing Prayer." Jacob prevailed over conditions with his idea of what God ought to be and do. The "man" with whom he "wrestled all night till the morning," was his own idea of God. It is our privilege to see face to face our own idea of the Divine Being. It is our privilege to strengthen and empower that idea, with ability to prevail for us against our circumstances before we arrive among them.

If my idea of God is that he could — but will not — help me to be wise, free and at peace, I shall certainly handle that idea with every skill I can summon, to beg, drive or coax it to prevail against the follies that there is danger of my committing, against the limitations I am shutting myself into, against the pain I see ahead of me.

Nobody ever deals with any God higher than his own idea. A great many of us try to get our idea to work against the sun shining on the circus tent and horse race, but lo and behold, it rains on our prayer meeting, streaks the cathedral with lightning tracks, and leaves the circus and race course in happy weather. Then we roll up our eyes, clasp our vanquished fingers and murmur something about the "mysteries of Providence."

There is really no mystery about it. We were not good at empowering and nerving our idea of what the ruler of a world ought to be and do, which is all.

Here stands the "I" at the head of its mass of ideas. One of its ideas is its idea of God. Each "I" may infuse that idea with power enough to prevail over anything that confronts us. Jacob spent a whole night nerving and invigorating his idea of God with energy and skill to conquer Esau with. He felt that the task was a severe one. There is a saying that "a brother offended is harder to be won than a strong city." "Toward morning," he felt "a virtue going out" of his "I" into his "idea."

God Transcends Idea

Of course, if you and I do not take the trouble to run the virtue out of our "I" into our "idea," it is a poor, nerveless thing to meet "Esau" by any manner of means. It may be the spring and push of our personal mind and conduct, but God, the true God, transcends idea. He who has no idea of God, but knows that the "Great Fact" abides, will not feel that he must wrestle with "It" to make it smooth out his hard places for him. He will know it as the Entirely Unalterable, the Eternally Changeless. He will see that its works are eternal, unalterable, changeless, like itself.

He who has "Esau" to meet, viz., trials, may nerve any one of his ideas with his "I" substance and the next day have no trials at all. He will think God changed Esau's mind, and be grateful for the change — that is, he will think God's merciful kindness erased his trials. But no, it was only his skill in nerving his idea of God.

He was only practicing "Jacob." It was his battledore and shuttlecock of "suggestions." He played well. For all trials are formulated "suggestions." All victories over them are formulated "suggestions." God is not a "suggestion." He runs not in any race. He is against nobody and nothing. He is for nobody and nothing. He is the Impartial One. Jesus Christ preached this lesson in one text: *"Blessed are the poor in spirit for theirs is the kingdom."* (Matthew 5:3) He knew that their idea of God was that he is Spirit. The more they should empty themselves of their ideas, the more there would be left of them. Even the idea that God is Spirit gets set up finally as a fighting character, infused with ability to run against the trials well. Get free from it, or "pour," every poor, in it.

There is a doctrine of God very seldom enunciated, but called out by this chapter. We know first that the two ideas, "spirit and matter," are opposite terms. Our first lesson in metaphysics reads: "Matter is the unreal and temporal; Spirit is the real and eternal." Pantajali called these opposing ideas "pairs of opposites." The presentation of matter to spirit is the instant destruction of matter. If you wish to prove this, tell your brain that it is "spiritual, not material" a few times and see how clear and intelligent it will feel. Its weight will dissolve somewhat. Keep on with that talk to your brain, and it will become an entirely new instrument in the fingers of your language.

All To Become Spiritual

Now, then, this universe is to be seen as spiritual, entirely spiritual, by our whole race, so all our Bibles prophesy. But when it is seen as spirit, all spirit, and spirit is one of a "pair of opposites," how shall spirit know that it is spirit, since there is nothing to compare itself with? There is then at this point no spirit. Do you see this? Then you are "poor in spirit." It is a very free fact, is it not? It is "the handful of corn on the top of the mountain" of all the doctrines of the world.

Once Jesus preached that we must never "go down from the housetop" of our high and true knowledge of God "to take anything out of our house" full of ideas of God. He meant we were better off to keep our eye on the God who transcends our mass of ideas, and not try to work our ideas, Jacob like, to beat and push our way with.

While Jesus was in the garden and Mary was trying to touch him as a physical being, he told her she had not even yet turned her ideas to him as "spirit, not matter." So he said, *"Touch me not, for*

I have not yet ascended." (John 20:17) He gave the whole army of disciples a powerful treatment to turn their mind to the spirit entirely. This has always been called the "ascent of mind; the ascent of life."

The more spiritual your doctrine is, the more uplifted you will feel. If you wish to improve this, try reading over a few pages of the Bible, and then try reading some criticisms upon it. The book will cure your spine, relieve your pain, inspire you with courage. The criticism will pin your spine stiff, increase your pain, depress your heart.

One is the "ascent to the Father;" the other is the "prowl among tombs."

Jesus Christ said, "Woe unto them that are" swelled up with worldly schemes when this wonderful doctrine shall stream from on high like the lightning. They shall be so cumbered with their own former ideas they cannot run, they cannot fly. So now, *"Blessed are the poor in spirit,"* for they can ascend. They do not try to compel an idea to run ahead, like a battering ram, against poverty. They know there is no poverty. They do not try to believe that spirit is victorious over matter. They know that that is only another attempt of ideas to fight ideas. They do not attempt to put spirit against matter to dissolve matter. That which they call spirit, lo, it is but their idea still.

Ideas Opposed to Each Other

They have a houseful of ideas, but now that they are on the housetop of knowledge that ideas of good, ideas of spirit, are nothing but pairs of opposites engaged in combat, they do not use any of them. *"They rest from their labors and their works do follow them."* (Revelation 14:13) They know what that means: *"My spirit shall not strive."* (Genesis 6:3)

When the strife was over, Jacob saw God; not while the strife was on. If we have ceased from trying to make our ideas win among the battalions of ideas now ranging the fields of universal mind, we are ready to see that the morning of God hath dawned on our face.

That which transcends ideas — that is God. It is no wonder that the Brahmins taught restraint of thoughts, even to stopping them entirely, that truth might shine full on their faces. Our own Bible teaches, *"Be still and know that I am God."* (Psalms 46:10)

So I must understand that it was deep night with me while I was thinking I had hardships to meet which my idea of God would overcome if I would work it faithfully. It was past midnight on the way toward morning when I saw that there were no hardships, for free spirit had dissolved them. It is nearing dawn when I am willing to be poor in spirit. It is glad sunshine when I recognize the presence of One against whom there is no opposite pitted; even in name. That One is indeed now present.

There is no doubt about great "works following" all who recognize what is now here in its unalterableness. The unalterable must manifest itself everywhere. When the doctrines of opposites are ended, mind rests from its labors and its works do follow it. Jacob expressed it in Verse 30: *"I have seen God and my life is preserved."*

Inter-Ocean Newspaper, April 1, 1894

LESSON XII

Discord In Jacob's Family

Genesis 37:1-11

The knowledge of truth is our Canaan. "Jacob dwelt in the land where his father was a stranger." Take the knowledge of that truth that sickness is unreality. When you know it, what transpires in your bodily condition? One little malady disappears, or a great one vanishes, according to whether you appreciate the truth much or little.

If you are one who appreciates that truth keenly, you will dwell in it. Some more statements of truth will be needed to feed your mind, to warm and nourish its other possibilities.

"I do not understand it," whine certain ones when told that disease is chimera, like the blindness of Charcot's subjects. By and by, they agree that it is so. They are dwelling within Canaan's borders. "I do not understand it," they whimper when told that poverty is as imaginary as disease. Directly, they discover that truth is not only *"God,*

74

thy health," (Jehovah-rapha - Jehovah makes whole) (Exodus 15:26), but *"God, thy provider" (Jehovah-jireh - Signifies the I AM provide*r), (Genesis 22:14). This pleases them and they are more firmly established in Canaan. They are Jacob preparing a Joseph with still further powerfulness.

For is the power of truth limited to saving you from shipwreck, healing you of rheumatism, clothing and feeding you? Nay, your knowledge of the stars that wheel in their orbits, of the shape of this planet, of the fourth dimension in space, will spring up like a seed long buried in a mummy case exposed to sunshine if you proclaim that matter is unreality, for the substance that will not permit anything but itself to exist is not matter.

It is wonderful how many unused powers lie ready to rise in bright splendor within you if you are bold enough to insist that there is only one mind, one substance, one power. Jacob set aside the law of punishment for sin by boldly ignoring sin in a fashion quite like the way the spiritual teachers of our time ignore disease.

Setting Aside Limitations

You may set aside limitation of any sort by boldly insisting that limitation is an unreal fence. *"I set before you an open door which no man can shut,"* said Jesus Christ. (Revelation 3:8)

If you are a patient or subject of Charcot, he tells you that your right foot is amputated. This causes you to limp. What sets you free? Knowledge

that he is lying to you. If you are a subject or patient of the doctors of divinity, what idea has
fenced off your powers and keeps you limping like
one with his foot gone?

You know very well that these doctors are honestly convinced we are all *"conceived in sin and
born in iniquity;"* (Psalms 51:5) *"Born to trouble as
the sparks fly upward;"* (Job 5:7) *"Born to wax old
like a garment;"* (Isaiah 50:9) "Born to die;" subject
to disease; liable to err; some of us were born with
little or no brains; some with much brains; some
are cowards, some are thieves, some are brave and
honest by inheritance, and some have their
clutches on the necks of their fellow men. But I say
unto you, these ideas are as false as Charcot's
information that a potato is an apple, or a peach is
an onion. I proclaim that the knowledge of what
Jesus Christ is will set every one of these ideas
aside and show us all alike wonderful in wisdom,
strength and majesty.

Jesus Christ is that body of true principles
which, when you once know them, will show you
forth as a being not dependent upon brains for
your understanding, and wholly independent of
the favor of the human race for your opportunities.
You will, by this set of principles, succeed in brilli-
ancy of wisdom and entire absolution from old age,
death and error.

If Jacob could "dwell in the land wherein his
father Isaac was a stranger," (Verse 1) you also

may dwell in a land of mind wherein your fathers were strangers.

"These are the generations of Jacob," (Verse 2) the prince of Israel. That is, whoever stands up and insists on truth independent of mortal suggestions, will see wonderful demonstrations. We "generate" manifestations by taking hold of our princehood. If I agree to one single proposition against my intelligence, I refuse my royalty of intelligence which was with me with God before the world was.

<u>"Whom Shall I Believe?"</u>

Jesus Christ says, *"I will give thee a mouth and wisdom which thine adversary shall not gainsay nor resist."* (Luke 21:15) But you tell me I cannot hold my own on this globe if the masters and the scholars set out to quench me. Whom shall I believe?

"I will destroy both the master and the scholar," said the Lord. (Malachi 2:12) Why? Because they "generate" on the side of "Bilhah and Zilpah." It is "Bilhah and Zilpah" who insist that man is dependent on brains for his intelligence and on opportunities of money or birth or personal excellences or agreement with reigning creeds for his getting on with mankind.

He needs nothing of the kind. He gets on most smoothly who takes truth just as it is. He who sees that intelligence fills the universe and brains are but statements of absence and presence thereof, declines the statement of absence and makes the statement of impartial presence. He takes his wisdom first hand. He faces all wisdom. "How hath this man letters, having never learned?"

He who sees that love fills the universe and that hearts are but statements of absence and presence theory, declines the statements of absence of love and makes the statement of impartial presence of love. He takes love at first hand. He faces all love. "How hath this man love, having never loved and never been loved?"

He who sees that goodness fills the universe and that convicts and tramps are but statements of absence thereof, declines the statement of absence of goodness; he may have been a tramp; he may have been a Joliet convict, but he then faces up the one impartial goodness. "How hath this man goodness, never having been good?"

Who are you shut up there in the reform school or tied to the typewriter? Do you not know that those things are but hypnotic stupors into which you are fenced by nodding your unconscious assent to the doctrines of men? Ho! Every one that thirsteth, to drink of the wells of his own love of freedom! Why do you take for your portion anything less than the free God? Have you not heard, have you not read, have you not known, that "I shall be satisfied when I awake?" And what shall wake up the seemingly stupid subjects of error?

On the Side of Truth

When the light that lighteth every man is proclaimed, there arise certain ones who "generate" or demonstrate on the side of truth. They are free from mistakes, free from poverty, free from disease, they understand their own worth in the universe. No man can shut down on their time. No man can shut down on their happiness. No man can shut down on their opportunities. Without friends they, by a new process, befriend the race. Without home, they shelter the world. Without possessions, they invest us all because they tell the truth. Truth shows us who we are, where we live, what we are doing. Truth sets us going on smooth pathways of life. Every other doctrine shall bow as Joseph's brothers' corn sheaves to the doctrine of the impartial omnipotent God in all men alike.

Every other doctrine shall bow, though once they were all in all to mankind as it is here proclaimed that even the sun and stars bowed down to Joseph, who in this lesson stands for young, newly spoken, advance truths about each man's own self.

"Joseph" means "he will add." So truth will indeed "add" new discovery after new discovery of your own wonderfulness. Now it is written that "Joseph's brethren envied him, but his father observed the saying." The astronomer thinks you must study stars for knowledge of stars, but Jesus Christ says, "Seek God and your knowledge of stars will transcend all that the brethren among star gazers declare." In old time language, they are "envious" at such an idea; in new time language, their stories are vanished myths like the diseases of those who have found out the truth about health.

Whoever watcheth his own inner light is Jacob, the Father. The reigning sectarian says Christ was buried and rose, but the "inner light" of truth as the Quakers who "observed the saying" shed its first beams on the doctrines of men, said Christ never was buried and Christ never rose. And the "inner light" of the Quakers was truth, which was the glory you had with the father before you became hypnotized by nodding assent to the winds of the sayings that you are of the world to get on with the world; that you must stay bound at the stake of your present lot till something transpires.

That "something" has transpired if you are ready, like Joseph in this 37th of Genesis, to tell boldly to "the sons of Bilhah and Zilpah," who are all the hypnotizers of our race, through schools, trades, religions, art, language, that you are not subject to them, though younger than they are (being, as it here says, only "seventeen years of age," which is the age at which truth keepeth her proclaimers forever and ever; herself being immortal youth), for you shall put their information under your feet, whether they fight well and long or yield now.

To know God is sure healing. To know God is sure support. To know God is sure protection. To know God is enough education, enough property, enough liberty.

Inter-Ocean Newspaper, April 8, 1894

LESSON XIII

Joseph Sold Into Egypt

Genesis 37:23-36

Strychnine, cocaine, arsenic are excellent tonics for people who have not learned the principle of inhaling vigor-producing mental ethers. Hate, enmity, curses are quickening tonics for minds that would easily lie back on tears of self-complacency.

Therefore, Jesus, the teacher, said much in praise of hate. *"Do good to them that hate you."* For this makes them hate your harder, and hate is the only medicine that will teach you how self-poised you can be. Every mind ought to be self-sustaining, self-inspiring. The mother hen, the mother cat, the mother eagle, understand this principle and practice it wisely.

Men and women practice this method of invigorating our intelligence without the conscious judgment of explaining why they are doing it.

They are as wonderfully led to hate us as the maternal fowl to rage against her offspring.

"Love your enemies." Why? Because they are producing chemical changes in the atmosphere round about your mind that will awaken it to knowledges you have no imagination of.

Get all the enemies you can by affirming omnipotent truth. "Blessed are ye" when, because of some mighty truth uttered by you years in advance of its acceptance by men, they "cast you into a pit," as the brethren did Joseph.

The fewer friends you have, the less effeminate your mind. It now leans on nothing. It is "woe to them that lean on the arm of flesh." Why? Because friends, money, adoring acquaintances are not something to lean upon, but something that hide the almighty arm of God.

So this lesson is a panorama of the history of one bold truth never swerved from when once uttered. Joseph means "he will add." Uttered truth is self-creative. Whatever you hear in the night watches, tell the world of it in the sunshine. Joseph saw and heard that he was a royal, a transcendent being, under whose feet the old creeds would fall. He told this aloud. The young truth glowed and transfigured and he never hung his head with regret of speaking it.

Yet he was not strong, nor brilliant because of it, till he was well hated. At the first dash of hate he stands utterly alone, fatherless, brotherless,

friendless. Now he is for the first time alive with
the spirit of what he has spoken. Now, for the first
time, he realizes his own godhead. It is no wonder
Jesus said, "Love your enemies," for their whispers
are vitalizing, their shouts are inspiring. Chemically compounding them with our truth, we realize
we are buoyed up and excited to utter grander
truths.

Influence on the Mind

How good, how divine, is the alchemy of hate
and cursing when the mouth has proclaimed a
truth! If the mind were dull and negative before, it
brightens and gleams with splendid fires now.

> *"He who hath led me to this way*
>
> *Still on the way will show;*
>
> *He who hath taught me of this way*
>
> *Still more will make me know."*

The Ishmaelites coming from Gilead, going
down into Egypt, bought Joseph of his brothers.

> *"But yesterday and Caesar might have stood
> against the world,*
>
> *Now none so poor to do him reverence."*

But it was the unfriended Joseph whose greatness dignifies the pages of human history. It is
Caesar's name that stands boldly forth on the tab-
lets of unwritten names of those that failed him in
his extremity. What is today's desolation but energy and brightness to that woman, that man, who
knows one truth, and that one truth proclaimed

has made his mind from that moment into another quality?

One does not need to keep his audible words continually going in order to generate hate. Thinking, realizing his inborn nobility, his rights in the universe, will breed it if one appreciates that it is because he came forth from heaven and brings God with him that he is a wonderful being.

The story of Joseph is the story of the "I AM" in any man when it is announced. Good works will not commend to courteous conduct. The brethren hated Joseph while he was serving them. It was not for being a good healer that they persecuted Jesus, but "because thou being a man makest thyself God."

Ishmael many years before Joseph's time, had been fed and strengthened in the wilderness by a miracle wrought through the chemistry of hate, and the note of payment came partially due to Abraham's descendant, Joseph, in the pit, and was entirely paid when Joseph fed his father and his brethren being utterly restored in honor.

Ishmael means, "Whom God hears." The God in Joseph caused his ears to hear the tramp of the traders' cattle and horsemen. No matter if we have to serve at trades and seem to be earning our bread like common slaves. Never mind if we have spoken of our inheritance from the all-owning God, and are still working at the counter or sewing machine. This is being Joseph. The day comes when we are the king's right hand.

Of Spiritual Origin

When we do not see any other way to do, only just as we are now doing for making our living, it is our ears hearing the Ishmaelites tramping. We hear the sounds of commerce, the ways of the trades, and are compelled to work in them. Let us know our mind. Is it a slave, or does it remember its origin? With the unquenchable truth that we are of spiritual origin, spiritual body, and spiritual power, we may work on till our miraculous genius breaks all bounds as Joseph's did when he stood before Pharaoh, King of Egypt, who exclaimed in awe: *"Can we find such a one as this is, a man in whom the spirit of God is?"* (Genesis 41:38) *"See, I have set thee over all the land of Egypt."* (Genesis 41:41)

This is all figurative. Egypt means "material things." Learning, art, science, manufactures: over all these the spiritually minded shall reign. The spiritually minded are now the meek of the earth, whose hour is striking to shortly take utter possession thereof.

Genesis and Revelation clasp hands on the sacred prophecy that in one hour shall the love of money, which now is "chief city," "queen of the world," be utterly prostrated and the kingdom of Zion be set up. Cannot every sovereign, every subject, be bought for gold? Therefore, his love of money is his queen, his king. His silent protest, his silent thought that with God no money consideration counts, is his meek idea, his Joseph, which as the people all get nearer and nearer one mind through international dealings, comes nearer and nearer to breaking out.

Do you not feel the great protest of the inner heart of mankind against putting us all to the service of money? Revelation promises freedom. Jesus promises freedom. Daniel promises freedom. Joseph prefigures freedom.

It is not gold itself, money itself, that is queen of the world, but love of money for what it has risen in our day to buy. Have you not read in the Book of Revelation how this love that has seduced men shall suddenly slip out of the mind of the race "in one hour," and the merchantmen, shipmen, buyers, and traders shall lament because buying and selling shall nevermore be upon the earth?

There is a way of living, which is not by the machinery of money, but by the divine proclamation of the silent protest now rapidly unifying itself. When this long-silent, meek "I AM that I AM" breaks forth, quickened by hate through ages, enlarged because uncherished through generations, empowering itself while said by all the world to be dead, mourned by the church as devoured, the heavens shall roll away as a scroll, the elements shall melt with fervent heat, "Zion awakes, redeemed without money" — Jesus is here. This is what the story of Joseph, hated by his brethren, sold into Egypt, mourned by Jacob, rising master of the world, means. The reading of this truth by you, agreeing with it even in the meekest region of

your being, is clasping hands with the kingdom of
God now.

Inter-Ocean Newspaper, April 15, 1894

LESSON XIV

Object Lessons Presented In The Book Of Genesis

Genesis 41:38-48

Whoever wrote the Book of Genesis put great principles into object lessons. From this chapter, we learn that the man who breathes the atmosphere of the four accusations which "mortal mind" directs against him, and yet remembers that his real character is not anything less than God, after serving three years at breathing the fourth one, is acknowledged by all the world to be what he himself has been acknowledging.

It is the "natural," the "carnal," the "mortal" way to accuse mind, fourthly, of foolishness and ignorance, if it once proclaims and perseveres in believing that it came forth from "Spirit, not matter;" that its destiny is dominion over "the world, the flesh, and the devil."

The foolish and ignorant may neither speak in their own defense nor be regarded when speaking of or for their neighbors. Therefore, when you feel the breath of the fourth accusation blowing on your mind, keep silence. The beauty of Joseph was his three years' imprisonment in the white castle at Memphis, during which the inspiration of a commanding judgment was generated by his masterful silence.

The close confinement of yourself in the prison-house of your present circumstances, out of which you cannot seem to get, is on account of a supposed mistake you once made in conducting your affairs. While you are going through the straightenings caused by your supposed mistakes, do everything that comes in your way to do silently, patiently, communing with the God Presence only. The moment your mind gets all the information of uncomplaining silence, you will be set in authority over your circumstances.

Pharaoh, who represents material conditions, and men who judge by common sense, admits that it is only the Spirit of God in a man that can afford to be silent when appearances are all against him. *"God hath showed thee all this, there is none so discreet and wise as thou art."* (Verse 39)

Emerson says that great men are they who succeed in bringing other men around to their way of thinking after twenty years. What eternal principle have you believed in and guided your life by for fourteen years as Joseph, or twenty years as Emerson did?

That is not an eternal principle, which says, "I would like to be honest. I started out to be honest, but I found I must meet men on their own ground and beat them with their own weapons." This principle of action must end in sudden disappearance of your health, reputation, happiness. It has no inspiring life in it.

The principle that has unkillable life in it must be a Jesus Christ one. The author of Genesis proposes that we regard ourselves as Spirit, and look upon all things as good. If we so persist, we shall find ourselves to be onlookers at a set of picture plays figuring out our status on our own principles. Jesus of Nazareth took the principles of himself and God as identical, and all that was real were his words. Nothing else amounted to anything at all. "Profiteth nothing," he said.

Joseph took the principle that he had no need to be agreeing with church or state or school dicta. He was transcendent being, needing not that any man should teach him books that he might know books, needing not to earn money or inherit it to be rich, needing not to practice a system of great thoughts to have a masterful mind. He took the simple stand of his own God-being. He stood there fourteen years and all Egypt shouted: *"Abreck! Abreck!" which means "Rejoice! Rejoice!" or as here translated, "We bow the knee."* (Verse 43)

Three years of that time he was in a tight place. In Psalms 105:17-18, we read that the fetters on his feet hurt him sorely, but he did not complain. Part of that time he was in a pit. Ten years he was a slave of Potiphar, captain of the guard of Pharaoh. All because he discovered that he was not flesh, but spirit; not carnal nature, but God nature from first to last; and never yielded his point!

This is the only greatness, then, a principle secretly maintained. It attends to its people when it gets ready. And it never fails to attend to its people at the right moment exactly.

"And Pharaoh called Joseph's name Zaphenath-paneah; and he gave him to wife Asenath, the daughter of Potiphera, priest of On."

"Zaphenath-paneah" means "Governor of the living One." Twice seven years the boy had served the high statement, "I am governor over material things by my spiritual prerogatives," as his father, Jacob, had served twice seven years for Rachel. "Fourteen" is a mystic number consecrated to patience. One cure in metaphysics represents our "patience" quality. It is the cure of our state of subordination to the dictum of associates. A bodily cure accompanies it. The moment we get away from the chain of silent endurance, we are new creatures. A new set of circumstances arises. A new bodily vigor seizes us.

At this point, Jesus made a whip and whipped the traders like a master in a southern cotton field. It was a wise chastising. Only one who had been set free from patience by serving patience could possibly strike me wisely with a whip of cords. Only one who came forth from God and understood the cure of leprosy, the raising of Lazarus instantaneously, could afford to call me a "scribe, Pharisee, hypocrite." An imitator of the "Master of Denunciation" makes bungling work of it. He has some sickness strike him to make him as an imitator. He has to turn and twist financially. The "Master of Denunciation" is governor of finances in the sight of all men. He is a handsome exhibition of the brilliant smiles of health through and through. Not till you understand raising the dead and turning poverty and hunger into plenty are you ready to chastise, call names, run down your fellow man scientifically.

The Old Testament lessons are exceedingly practical. They corroborate by actual histories the principles announced by Jesus Christ. We may take them on the extremely material plane and be benefited by studying them. We may take them on the mental or intellectual plane, or by ideas, and we see how to run our minds with more skillfulness. We may take them on the plane of regarding ideas of mind and physical movements as both equally chimerical and symbolic, and stand aside from the universe free as the Changeless One.

On the plane of ideas, we are told by this Bible section, that a mystic beauty steals over the face and form after a high statement has been held its rightful length of time. It is told by "giving Joseph Asenath" the favor of Isis. When Isis is unveiled for the whole world's vision, the world's beauty is eternal. Nothing fades and grows unsightly.

Beautiful presence of the spirit in our midst is Isis, the Holy Spirit of God. Any eternal truth secretly maintained will cause it to beautify our faces with the light of its presence visibly. Did not Jesus Christ say that whoever would make his name their breath as the priests of On inhaled and exhaled Isis-Osiris, and as Brahmins inspired and expired Om, would have the Holy Spirit? What is so wonderful as the Holy Spirit? Its fine fire radiance is the mystic breath which understanding of our own spirit gives. Whosoever has the Holy Spirit through Christian science lessons is master of the corn and the gold of all earth. Whosoever gives up his high statements before he has given them the Joseph service has no more masterfulness over the poverty, the hunger, the unequal distribution, the debts, the panics of this age than he had before he used them.

"By their fruits ye shall know them." (Matthew 7:20) The hour pushes close. Many a voice urges us to let go of the truths which Jesus said keep. This lesson of Joseph comes floating over the centuries from the land of the Sphinx and the pyramids, from the city of On, where priestly love of art never equaled the splendor hinted at of what the Holy Presence would work for mankind when Jesus should be born with a name within whose folded sounds is bread for the world without money and without price.

Did you ever believe that it was folly to make a spiritual affirmation high out of the reach of your personal experience, but hold it through fair and foul, dark and light, friendship and enmity, till it should take you on its own wings whither it would?

If not, then you have not seen what the story of Joseph signifies. You have put aside the authority of Jesus, "keep my sayings"; you are easily tempted. You are of them that the prophets promised who should say in these days, "What profit?" and "Where is the Lord?" The cure you want to see accomplished is the one which patience only, and that on your own part, will work out. Nobody will work the cure for you, which stands for your own proposition, steadfastly, silently maintained. Nobody can breathe for you. The patience may not be required for fourteen years as we reckon time, but it certainly is past the span where you are seemingly in need of a friend, and those who seem wisest dispute the wisdom of your course past and present, because you seem to be in the prison of misfortune. Joseph judged not by appearance. Though he stood alone, he was not alone. The Lord, of whom he had been speaking, to whom, as within himself he had been speaking, suddenly appeared as a master.

"Who could abide the day of his coming?" (Malachi 3:2) Could famine stay in Joseph's sight? Could friendlessness be a state of his life? Could

those whom he knew, friend and foe, be poverty stricken?

In this hour the "famine of the land" can be outwitted only by high statements concerning your own divinity, from which you do not swerve till their light breaks over your life and your omnipotent spirit takes possession.

Inter-Ocean Newspaper, April 22, 1894

LESSON XV

"With Thee Is Fullness Of Joy"

Genesis 45:1-15

There is a mental chemistry and there is a material chemistry. A "chemical" is that "resulting from the operation of the forces upon which composition and decomposition depend, as chemical changes, chemical combinations." (Webster's definition)

In material combinations of substance we find two ingredients uniting and making what might be called annihilation. Camphor gum and alcohol unite and no extra space is required. Ether and the alcohol then unite with air, and there is nothing visible left. Lo! Anger of mind and repentance unite, and only the repentance is left. Repentance of mind exposed to the sunshine of forgiveness, and what is left? What so ethereal as pure joy? This, at its supreme is God, the sun and breath of the universe.

99

On this plan of explaining Brahman, the Oriental philosopher declares that all substance in the universe can unite chemically and occupy only a mathematical point, and that all the states of mind now filling the universe may chemically unite and make the God Mind, which is the "inconceivably small one," the "one point."

Instead, then, of teaching us to "watch for God omnipresently external, the mystic Easterner tells us to focus our mind to an inconceivably fine point, till all our angers, criticisms, griefs, loves, hates are — by the chemistry of mind — resolved into the one unnamable center.

The attention of thousands upon thousands of intelligent and noble men and women is being called to this manner of resolving all things into divinity. If I would be entirely fair in my interpretations of these Bible lessons, I must turn over the leaves of every genuine book of spiritual teachings that I can lay my hands on and report those explanations which have been accepted by the wise and sincere of all ages as practicable.

India Favors Philosophic Thought

Max Muller, in *What Can India Teach Us?* says: "If I were asked under what sky the human mind has most fully developed some of its choicest gifts, has most deeply pondered on the greatest problems of life, and has found solutions of some of them which will deserve the attention even of those who have studied Plato and Kant, I should point to India."

Today's Bible lesson teaches the chemistry of repentance and forgiveness. It brings forth joyousness. With these chemical writings, prosperity is manifest. Thus on the mental plane, a state of mind is promised to compel material operations. Joy has a charm about it to attract good luck.

Grief has a charm about it to attract misfortune. Socrates taught this. The Bible teaches it.

Sometimes the Bible shows that we run into the consequences of our former states of mind. The envy of Joseph's brethren ran into Joseph of Heliopolis.

What a demonstration took place; the eastern philosopher would see the clash of the good and the evil state of mind. The materialist would see only that Joseph outwitted his brethren.

Sometimes, the one point of Being, which is divinity, is called a lightning spark. It is said to be the center of every man's being. When a man's mind thinks like the God at his center, he demonstrates healing power like Jesus; he demonstrates prosperity for his neighbors like Joseph.

Sometimes, these laws of thoughts are explained by metaphysicians by geometrical symbols, as angles and circles and points. Pythagoras said that "God geometries." For instance, as a horizontal line meets a perpendicular and makes a right angle, so a right purpose in the heart touches the everlasting purpose of God and a noble character appears in the world's life.

What These Figures Impart

This is neither foolish nor wicked language of explanation where a noble purpose, a high evangel is intended by these figures of speech: "Who are these that lie in wait for the righteous to condemn them for a word?"

"And Joseph said unto his brethren: Be not grieved or angry with yourselves that ye sold me hither, for God did send me before you to preserve life." (Verse 5) Here is the denial of sin. "God is too pure to behold iniquity." He who is most like God sees less sin. When his mind comes in contact with sin, it annihilates it. Only one mind is left. This can be applied to the gambler, the embezzler, the fratricide. There is an association of mind, which results in one mind. Joseph had got his mind so potent after twenty-two years of training that he was able to make wickedness dissolve in his presence like camphor gum in alcohol.

In metaphysical healing, you will find that you cannot cure a case of dropsy if you hate the sensuality of the man who lugs the dropsy. Neither can you cure him of sensuality while it is so real to you. The mind of you is not trained like Joseph's. You must go on somewhat longer thinking of the divine spark in all men, till a moment arrives when the divine in man is all that you see in all men. Then the dropsy man with his veil of sensuality will not be visible. His God nature will be plain in your sight. This will cure him.

Suppose it takes you twenty-two years of concentrated attention to the divine in man to realize it? Joseph took twenty-two years to train his mind to dissolve the iniquity of his brothers. In his sight, they were no longer wicked.

Now, while we hang and imprison our fellowmen for crimes, we see that we have no heads of state who have spent twenty-two years thinking so constantly of the divinity in all men that when the crimes appear in their presence a chemical change transpires, leaving only the divine.

The Errors of Governments

Heads of state try to imitate the chemistry of godliness by hangings, guillotines, electricity, imprisonment for life, etc. This seems to leave their minds alive and alone on the boards of human action. The criminals are annihilated. Age after age of this kind of chemistry has been going on. Has it lessened embezzlers, seducers, gamblers?

The imitation of truth and methods of annihilation must remain forever unsuccessful. Only the true is successful. Joseph is able to say, *"So now, it was not you, but God."* (Verse 8) Our heads of state must be able to say this.

About once in so long, a great famine seizes upon every nation. In our country it is always a money famine. It is always visible when the greedy mind of the nation faces up some new religious idea that is gaining ground.

Once it was the idea that there are no black or white in Christ Jesus. Then it was that all have an equal right to health. This day's famine comes from the religious proclamation that all men are equally divine with Jesus Christ. The proposition started out over the mental atmospheres when greed was great.

Thus did Joseph's great proposition, "I am God," start out when the greed of Israel's people waxed great. After twenty-two years, they collided. Joseph's proposition had unkillable substance in it. The brethren's greed of gain, greed of fame, greed of power, disappeared. Hath not a whole world waxed greatly greedy altogether today? Hath the idea that "God in man is his only substance" ability to annihilate greed in a whole world? I am sure that it has. All Bibles prophecy that there shall be finally one kingdom only left on earth.

From India, with her One Point, whose name is Brahman; from Arabia, with her One Presence, whose name is Allah; from Egypt, with her Father-Mother Nourisher of all, whose name is Osiris-Isis; from Persia with her Shining Light whose name is Ormuzed (or Oromasdes, the Grecianized form of the Zoroastrian deity, Ahura-Mazda); from Palestine, with her everlasting Word, which is God; we get the same scientific calculation: in that day shall the God of harmony set up a kingdom which shall consume all other kingdoms.

There is no harmony like the knowledge that not only is the preacher who speaks what the church papers approve divine from center to circumference, but Prendergast also is divine in all extent.

If it takes twenty-two years of attention to this One Point, to be able to dissolve or annihilate iniquity, I shall then and there only be Joseph, capable head of state.

Inter-Ocean Newspaper, April 29, 1894

LESSON XVI

Change Of Heart

Genesis 50:14-26

Joseph had practiced one state of mind twenty-two years. Whenever he came into the immediate presence of other people of an opposite state of mind to his own, a chemical change occurred.

Eleven criminals (his brethren) stood in a row before him while he was governor of Egypt, and such was the mental suffering of them that while the chemistry of resolving their mind state into his was transpiring, they wept aloud and cried, *"Forgive us our trespass."* (Verse 17)

"And Joseph wept when they spoke unto him." (Verse 17)

One point of last Sunday's lesson is reviewed in Verse 17 of this one, viz., no man is fitted to be a governor of state until his mind has been trained to chemicalize the criminal classes so that by contact with him, they repent in honest humiliation as before God.

Whoever as a criminal is thus prostrated, has one everlasting truth for his consolation: "Their sins will I remember no more against them."

All religious teachings have this one intention of making nothing of sinfulness by a state of mind. They do not urge jails, reformation, poor houses; no, but change of heart. And the change of heart they urge over and over is produced by two processes:

    a) First, by taking an aphorism (a concisely stated truth) opposite to the experience and holding it as a persistent thought till the mind is set to it as an instrument is set to a key-note, as Joseph did.

    b) Second, by coming into direct contact with such a mind as every head of state is supposed to have (according to religion), "and suffering the swift change of heart which had been likened to the fermentation of acid and alkali mingling in a chemist's jar, as Joseph's eleven brothers did; as the thief on the cross did.

When an aphorism has wrought its mission, you will discover that to you there is no sin in the heart of your fellowman. Then if you say this aloud to those who do not accept or have not practiced whispering your aphorism, they immediately accuse you of licensing iniquity.

Religion As A Science

It is high time that religion were taught as a science. The error in a preacher's reasoning is discoverable quickly if you know the twelve points of science taught in all Bibles alike.

Which is better, to hang a man or change his heart? How do you change his heart? By being in the opposite state of heart yourself. If you are in a state of heart where his crime is crime to you, what is the difference between your point of view and his?

Just in matter of like and dislike. That is all. He likes it. You do not. The crime is as real a transaction to your sight as his.

But religion teaches that the right view is not to judge after the sight of the eyes nor after the hearing of the ears. The God state of mind is to see God and nothing else than God every where, every instant.

"He beholdeth not iniquity," Joseph finally arrived at this state. Jesus was there all the time. If this religion irritates you, it is a sign that you are experiencing a chemical change. If you call it a sophistry (deceptive reasoning) or license to sin, you are being secretly undermined in your present religious views. Soon you will believe this very word. You cannot help it any more than the eleven criminals arrayed before Joseph could help repenting.

Notice in this lesson that Joseph promises to nourish the eleven criminals and their little ones (Verse 21) because they were meek, which having done for over fifty years he chose to dwell in another realm where he could work out the proposition, "there is no death." He had finished the work belonging to his one idea, "I am supreme."

There is no record of any having yet taken the proposition, "There is no death," and turning their minds so to it that they are now visibly among us, being, as reckoned by years, over 100 or so. Some, however, left no material remains when they departed, as Moses, Elijah, Enoch. On this subject, Joseph was silent indeed. He agreed with the rest of the world and at the age of 110 (Verse 26) he said, *"I die ... and ye shall carry up my bones from hence."* (Verses 24-25)

On this subject, Jesus said much and is now often visible to mankind, intending to be shortly visible to all men alike, His mystic treatments having fulfilled their purpose.

<u>The Number Fourteen</u>

This lesson repeats the name Joseph fourteen times. When a Bible chapter repeats a name many times, its intention is to give us a metaphysical treatment on the line, which the name signifies.

Fourteen is a number consecrated to double fulfillment. Your own mind is set to a six day's task and then rest on its seventh day. The appearance of your world is changed by six day's performances, and on the seventh satisfies you with changeless perfection.

Each aphorism held in mind has six actives and one still. It moves on nature's face to make things demonstrate to prove itself. All the aphorisms of religious science are twelve. They all make the same round of change. He who can concentrate the meaning of the whole twelve statements of religious science into one is able to accomplish wonders quickly. Peter converted 3,000 by one lesson. He was already convinced himself and compelled conviction easily.

When certain Orientals wish you to receive the mental treatment of a word, they tell you to draw in your breath and repeat the word, hold the breath repeating the word; exhale the breath repeating the word.

This lesson from the Orient has the same secret purpose when it repeats the word, which means that your forgiving spirit shall increase, and increase while your attention is fixed upon it in the form of a story. The book of Genesis is an old-fashioned novel with a "motif."

Paracelsus said that reading the book of Revelation over and over would stimulate and draw forth your hidden magical powers.

By magical powers, he meant those unused faculties of man whereby he can heal by thought at a distance, stop crimes by his eyes, illuminate a room by a turn of his hand, as the adept did for Hensoldt, the German traveller, and many other performances without material aid.

So the story of Joseph stimulates the forgiving spirit and enlarges and increases your influence for good. It is quite a chemical change to the unforgiving chord in your mind. It is a chemical change to your inferiority among your fellowmen. It is impossible to read the story of Joseph from beginning to end without finding yourself more or less enlarged in the estimation of your fellowbeings.

Thus the story of Joseph has for part of its "motif," your high place in the estimation of mankind.

A certain youth who had never read the Bible till he was eighteen years of age exclaimed:

"Why, it is a book of magic! Look here, now, you read over and over an obscure passage and suddenly you are wide awake with a new piece of information, which the passage has not alluded to. You are told to watch a white or blue lily of the field and a new way of making your living will be shown you. The ant is a microscope to convey wisdom, though ostensibly to set you hustling. The lightning watched shall cause your thoughts to demonstrate instantly. Even the sentence, *'as the lightning shineth from the east unto the west,'* (Matthew 22:27) has the effect of a metaphysical change to make you do something promptly."

Divine Magicians

Moses, Elisha, Daniel, Jesus, were magicians of a divine sort of whom the mighty Chaldean sorts were spurious imitators. There do indeed seem to be legitimate processes of bringing things to pass by a set to of the mind. I do not wonder that the metaphysicians have said, "Mind is God." Mind "will bring out just as much if drawn upon by Coxey and his crew, as if drawn upon and marched out by Napoleon. It is not the outward appearance that treats the race, but the "motif."

Another who investigated all the Bibles said they were all works on the magic of the divine mysteries. One man without eyeballs had his attention so transfixed by certain parts of the Christian Scripture that the eyeballs began to grow and the sight thereof to generate. Many have received to the magic of the name Jesus Christ oft-times repeated. All the majesty of Joseph, the sinewy endurance of Jewry, the prosperity of Abraham, the splendid diction of David, the knowledge of Solomon, are focused into it. *"In My Name shall the Gentiles trust."* (Matthew 12:21)

It changes the constitution and quality of each thought as it conies face to face -with it by repeating it silently. With its mysterious chemistry it transmutes poor, inferior, incompetent minds into noble beings, able to rise by the cross of ignominy into the adoration of a globe as in chariots of shiny gold across morning highways of fairer lands than sun ere shone on. *"The meek shall inherit the earth.* " (Matthew 5:5) None so meek as they who read the Scriptures over and over without attempting either to put their own construction upon them or trying to reconcile erudition with their seeming discrepancies. Who so meek as he that lets them do with him what they will? "Teach," said Jesus.

The inheritance of sons of kings is yours; the greatness of kings at their untold best is yours; the ascension on happy wings of light out of your present sorrow is yours who read in meekness.

Inter-Ocean Newspaper, May 6, 1894

Notes

Other Books by Emma Curtis Hopkins

- *Class Lessons of 1888 (WiseWoman Press)*
- *Bible Interpretations (WiseWoman Press)*
- *Esoteric Philosophy in Spiritual Science (WiseWoman Press)*
- *Genesis Series*
- *High Mysticism (WiseWoman Press)*
- *Self Treatments with Radiant I Am (WiseWoman Press)*
- *Gospel Series (WiseWoman Press)*
- *Judgment Series in Spiritual Science (WiseWoman Press)*
- *Drops of Gold (WiseWoman Press)*
- *Resume (WiseWoman Press)*
- *Scientific Christian Mental Practice (DeVorss)*

Books about Emma Curtis Hopkins and her teachings

- *Emma Curtis Hopkins, Forgotten Founder of New Thought –* Gail Harley
- *Unveiling Your Hidden Power: Emma Curtis Hopkins' Metaphysics for the 21st Century (also as a Workbook and as A Guide for Teachers) – Ruth L. Miller*
- *Power to Heal: Easy reading biography for all ages –Ruth Miller*

To find more of Emma's work, including some previously unpublished material, log on to:

www.highwatch.org
www.emmacurtishopkins.com

800. 603.3005

WISEWOMAN PRESS

Books Published by WiseWoman Press

By Emma Curtis Hopkins

- *Resume*
- *Gospel Series*
- *Class Lessons of 1888*
- *Self Treatments including Radiant I Am*
- *High Mysticism*
- *Esoteric Philosophy in Spiritual Science*
- *Drops of Gold Journal*
- *Judgment Series*
- *Bible Interpretations: series I, thru XIV*

By Ruth L. Miller

- *Unveiling Your Hidden Power: Emma Curtis Hopkins' Metaphysics for the 21st Century*
- *Coming into Freedom: Emily Cady's Lessons in Truth for the 21st Century*
- *150 Years of Healing: The Founders and Science of New Thought*
- *Power Beyond Magic: Ernest Holmes Biography*
- *Power to Heal: Emma Curtis Hopkins Biography*
- *The Power of Unity: Charles Fillmore Biography*
- *Power of Thought: Phineas P. Quimby Biography*
- *Gracie's Adventures with God*
- *Uncommon Prayer*
- *Spiritual Success*
- *Finding the Path*

Watch our website for release dates and order

www.wisewomanpress.com

List of
Bible Interpretation Series
with date from 1st to 14th Series.

This list is complete through the fourteenth Series. Emma produced about thirty Series of Bible Interpretations.

She followed the Bible Passages provided by the International Committee of Clerics who produced the Bible Quotations for each year's use in churches all over the world.

Emma used these for her column of Bible Interpretations in both the Christian Science Magazine, at her Seminary and in the Chicago Inter-Ocean Newspaper.

First Series

Second Series

Third Series

Fourth Series

Fifth Series

Sixth Series

Seventh Series

127

Eighth Series

128

Ninth Series

July 2 - September 27, 1893

Lesson 1	Secret of all Power	July 2nd
Acts 16: 6-15	The Ancient Chinese Doctrine of Taoism	
	Manifesting of God Powers	
	Paul, Timothy, and Silas	
	Is Fulfilling as Prophecy	
	The Inner Prompting.	
	Good Taoist Never Depressed	
Lesson 2	The Flame of Spiritual Verity	July 9th
Acts 16:18	Cause of Contention	
	Delusive Doctrines	
	Paul's History	
	Keynotes	
	Doctrine Not New	
Lesson 3	Healing Energy Gifts	July 16th
Acts 18:19-21	How Paul Healed	
	To Work Miracles	
	Paul Worked in Fear	
	Shakespeare's Idea of Loss	
	Endurance the Sign of Power	
Lesson 4	Be Still My Soul	July 23rd
Acts 17:16-24	Seeing Is Believing	
	Paul Stood Alone	
	Lessons for the Athenians	
	All Under His Power	
	Freedom of Spirit	
Lesson 5	(Missing) Acts 18:1-11	July 30th
Lesson 6	Missing No Lesson *	August 6th
Lesson 7	The Comforter is the Holy Ghost	August 13th
Acts 20	Requisite for an Orator	
	What is a Myth	
	Two Important Points	
	Truth of the Gospel	
	Kingdom of the Spirit	
	Do Not Believe in Weakness	

Tenth Series

October 1 – December 24, 1893

Lesson 1	*Romans 1:1-19*	October 1st
	When the Truth is Known	
	Faith in God	
	The Faithful Man is Strong	
	Glory of the Pure Motive	
Lesson 2	*Romans 3:19-26*	October 8th
	Free Grace.	
	On the Gloomy Side	
	Daniel and Elisha	
	Power from Obedience	
	Fidelity to His Name	
	He Is God	
Lesson 3	*Romans 5*	October 15th
	The Healing Principle	
	Knows No Defeat.	
	In Glorified Realms	
	He Will Come	
Lesson 4	*Romans 12:1*	October 22nd
	Would Become Free	
	Man's Co-operation	
	Be Not Overcome	
	Sacrifice No Burden	
	Knows the Future	
Lesson 5	*I Corinthians 8:1-13*	October 29th
	The Estate of Man	
	Nothing In Self	
	What Paul Believed	
	Doctrine of Kurozumi	
Lesson 6	*I Corinthians 12:1-26*	November 5th
	Science of The Christ Principle	
	Dead from the Beginning	
	St. Paul's Great Mission	
	What The Spark Becomes	
	Chris, All There Is of Man	
	Divinity Manifest in Man	
	Christ Principle Omnipotent	

Eleventh Series

January 1 – March 25, 1894

Lesson 1	*Genesis 1:26-31 & 2:1-3*	January 7th
	The First Adam	
	Man: The Image of Language Paul and Elymas	
Lesson 2	*Genesis 3:1-15*	January 14th
	Adam's Sin and God's Grace	
	The Fable of the Garden	
	Looked-for Sympathy	
	The True Doctrine	
Lesson 3	*Genesis 4:3-13*	January 21st
	Types of the Race	
	God in the Murderer	
	God Nature Unalterable	
Lesson 4	*Genesis 9:8-17*	January 28th
	God's Covenant With Noah	
	Value of Instantaneous Action	
	The Lesson of the Rainbow	
Lesson 5	I Corinthians 8:1-13	February 4th
	Genesis 12:1-9	
	Beginning of the Hebrew Nation	
	No Use For Other Themes	
	Influence of Noble Themes	
	Danger In Looking Back	
Lesson 6	*Genesis 17:1-9*	February 11th
	God's Covenant With Abram	
	As Little Children	
	God and Mammon	
	Being Honest With Self	
Lesson 7	*Genesis 18:22-23*	February 18th
	God's Judgment of Sodom	
	No Right Nor Wrong In Truth	
	Misery Shall Cease	
Lesson 8	*Genesis 22:1-13*	February 25th
	Trial of Abraham's Faith	
	Light Comes With Preaching	
	You Can Be Happy NOW	

Twelfth Series

Thirteenth Series

July 1 – September 30, 1894

Fourteenth Series

October 7 – December 30, 1894

2206869R00084

Made in the USA
San Bernardino, CA
23 March 2013